IRELAND

A CHRONOLOGY AND FACT BOOK

6000 B.C. - 1972

Compiled and Edited by
WILLIAM D. GRIFFIN

1973
OCEANA PUBLICATIONS, INC.
Dobbs Ferry, New York

Library of Congress Cataloging in Publication Data

Griffin, William D   comp.
        Ireland: 6000 B. C. - 1972; a chronology & fact
book.

(World chronology series)
Bibliography: p.
SUMMARY: A chronology of Irish history, emphasizing
its modern political events and containing pertinent
documents and statistics.
    1. Ireland-History--Sources. 2. Ireland --
History--Chronology. [1. Ireland--History]
I. Title.
DA905.G74   941.5   73-12694
ISBN 0-379-16302-0

Manufactured in the United States of America

TABLE OF CONTENTS

EDITOR'S FOREWORD

Ireland, small in size and population, isolated on the outer rim of
Europe, has none the less played no mean role in the development of West-
ern civilization. A refuge of scholars during the Dark Ages, she was for
generations the greatest missionary center in expanding Christendom. In
the days of her adversity, she sent forth adventurers and emigrants whose
energies built and enriched foreign lands from America to Australia.
Linked for 800 years in a complex, embittered relationship with her island
neighbor, she both contributed to England's achievements and consorted
with England's enemies, periodically asserting her nationhood, and peren-
nially engaging the interest of the world's statesmen.

If those nations are happy which have no history, then surely one of
the reasons for Ireland's sorrows is that she has too much. Burdened and
obsessed by their past, her people are haunted by old enmities and by dead
men whose unredressed grievances plague the living. The historian, at
least, can cast off some of the physical burden of so lengthy a history by
concentrating on certain phases of it. This book gives only limited attention to the glories of ancient Ireland and to the deeds of the Irish overseas,
and concentrates upon the modern period of Ireland's history, during which
her involvement with England forms a continuing theme. With the eyes of
the world now focused upon the climactic struggle in a centuries-old conflict, such an historical perspective should be all the more valuable.

The Chronology, accordingly, gives proportionately greater emphasis to the modern period of Irish political history, while the section of documents, which aims at illustrating some stages of that history, begins with
the Tudor attempt to impose direct rule during the sixteenth century. A
similar emphasis will be found in the Bibliography, though reference is
made there to works dealing fully with the earlier ages of Ireland's history,
and with her rich cultural heritage.

William D. Griffin
St. John's University

c. 6000 B.C.   First evidence of human habitation in Ireland.

c. 3000 B.C.   Farming and community life have developed in Ireland;
                 stone burial chambers ("megalithic tombs") constructed
                 by tribal groups.

c. 1500 B.C.   Mining and metal-working have developed to the point
                 where an overseas trade in gold and bronze ornaments
                 and weapons is being carried on.

c. 200 B.C.   Celts arrive in Ireland and establish their political and
                 cultural mastery over the earlier inhabitants.

A.D. 1 - 200   Heroic age of Irish saga tradition.

c. 300   Beginning of Irish raids against Roman Britain.

432   Traditional date of St. Patrick's arrival in Ireland to
                 preach Christianity.

500 - 550   Growth of Irish monasticism.

563   Saint Columba founds the monastery of Iona, from which
                 the evangelization of southern Scotland and northern Eng-
                 land is carried out.

590   Beginning of Irish missionary activity on the Continent.

c. 650   Great age of Irish monastic schools and production of
                 illuminated manuscripts.

c. 700   High point in Irish artistic production, masterpieces of
                 metal-working, e.g. the Tara Brooch, the Ardagh Chalice.

795   Beginning of Viking raids on Ireland.

c. 841   Dublin founded by Vikings, who begin to settle permanent-
                 ly in Ireland and found coastal settlements which grow in-
                 to the first cities in Ireland.

1002   Brian Boru, having overthrown all rival claimants and
                 subordinated the provincial kings, is acknowledged as
                 High-King of Ireland.

1014   Battle of Clontarf. Brian Boru defeats the Norsemen of
                 Dublin and their allies, ending the Viking power in Ireland,
                 but is himself killed.

1100-60   Growth in administrative organization and authority of
            the Church, marked by creation of territorial dioceses
            (1111), acknowledgment of archbishop of Armagh as pri-
            mate of all Ireland (1152). Antagonism between ecclesi-
            astical leadership and provincial kings.

1169   Norman invasion of Ireland under the leadership of Rich-
            ard FitzGilbert de Clare, Earl of Pembroke (May -
            August).

1170   Dublin captured by the Normans (September 21).

1171   King Henry II of England comes to Ireland and receives
            the homage of his Norman vassals, and of many Irish
            bishops and princes (October).

1175   Treaty of Windsor between Henry II and Rory O'Connor,
            ard-ri (high king), who is recognized as ruler of Connaught,
            in return for his acceptance of the English king as his
            overlord (October).

1200   Castles built by the Normans at Trim and Carrickfergus.
            These were the first of the hundreds of stone fortresses
            built by the invaders -- and later by the Gaelic magnates
            -- which are still a feature of the Irish countryside.

1210   King John visits Ireland, imposes royal authority on the
            Norman barons, and decrees that the laws and customs
            of England be observed in Ireland.

1235   Norman invasion of Connaught, aimed at bringing that
            still independent kingdom under English control.

1297   First meeting of the Irish Parliament.

1315   Invasion of Ireland by Edward Bruce, brother of King
            Robert of Scotland, at invitation of certain Irish lords.
            He is crowned high king, and ravages the English out-
            posts (1316-17).

1318   Battle of Faughart (October 14); Edward Bruce killed.

1348   Bubonic plague -- the "Black Death" -- sweeps through
            Ireland.

1366   Statutes of Kilkenny passed by Irish parliament.   English
       settlers in Ireland are forbidden to adopt Gaelic language,
       dress or customs, or to assimilate themselves in any
       way with the native population.

1399   Richard II in Ireland, seeking to impose his authority
       over the Gaelic lords; in his absence, Henry of Lancaster
       (Henry IV) usurps his throne.

1435   Privy Council of Ireland reports to the King that effective
       English rule does not extend beyond the Pale (the area
       centering on Dublin), and urges that the Pope be asked to
       preach a crusade against the rebellious Irish.

1449   Richard of York named Viceroy of Ireland. He estab-
       lishes in Ireland a loyalty to the Yorkist cause which
       will endure during the Wars of the Roses.

1462   Battle of Pilltown. Lancastrian forces, led by the Butler
       family, defeated by Yorkists, under the Earl of Desmond.
       Beginning of the ascendancy of the Fitzgeralds, Earls of
       Desmond and Kildare.

1478   Garret Mor Fitzgerald, the "Great Earl" of Kildare, es-
       tablishes himself as "uncrowned king" of Ireland.

1487   Lambert Simmel crowned in Christ Church Cathedral,
       Dublin. This pretender, backed by Yorkist nobles,
       claimed to be the nephew of Edward IV. He was recog-
       nized as King Edward VI by the Earl of Kildare and most
       of the other Irish nobles and prelates (March 24).

       Simmel and his army, including an Irish contingent led
       by Thomas Fitzgerald, the Earl's brother, defeated at
       Stoke, England, by Henry VII (June).

1491   Perkin Warbeck seeks support in Ireland, claiming to be
       Prince Richard of York. The Earls of Kildare and Des-
       mond support his pretensions, but do not offer open aid,
       and he leaves for France in 1492.

1494.   Meeting of "Poynings' Parliament" (to 1495). Summoned
       by the new Lord Deputy, Sir Edward Poynings, the Parlia-
       ment sought to reestablish firm royal authority in Ireland
       by a series of enactments, the most important of which
       was "Poynings' Law", which laid down the supremacy of
       the English crown, council, and parliament over the Irish
       legislature.

1513	Garret Og Fitzgerald succeeds his father as Earl of Kildare and "chief governor" of Ireland.
1534	Revolt of "Silken Thomas" (June). Thomas Fitzgerald, Baron Offaly, son of the Earl of Kildare, rebels against Henry VIII's efforts to restrain Fitzgerald power and extend royal authority. In the course of his rebellion, he also raises the banner of orthodox Catholicism in opposition to Henry's anti-Roman policy. Silken Thomas is captured in August 1535.
1536	Meeting of the "Reformation Parliament" (to 1537). Henry VIII is acknowledged "only Supreme Head on Earth of the whole church of Ireland", but the Reformation makes little headway outside of the Pale and the principal provincial towns. Execution of "Silken Thomas" and his five uncles, marking the end of the Kildare ascendancy.
1541	Irish Parliament proclaims Henry VIII King of Ireland, thus superceding the medieval title "Lord of Ireland" with one that asserts a more positive claim to sovereignty.
1542	The principal Irish chieftans surrender their claims to regal status and receive from Henry VIII English titles and grants as proprietors of their traditional clan lands under English property laws.
1549	Beginning of "plantations" in Leix and Offaly. These are designated as areas of English settlement, with the aim of extending effective English rule and "civilization" beyond the Pale (continuing through 1557).
1553-8	Under Mary I, Catholicism and Papal authority are reestablished in England and Ireland.
1558-60	Following accession of Elizabeth I, the Anglican Church is restored in England and Ireland.
1562	Shane O'Neill raises revolt against Elizabeth's government in Ireland.
1567	Shane O'Neill defeated and killed.

1568   First Desmond Rebellion (to 1572). Resistance to English rule in province of Munster by adherents of the Earl of Desmond. Appeals for aid to the Pope and the King of Spain bring little assistance, but establish a precedent.

1579   Second Desmond rebellion (to 1583). Instigated by the Earl of Desmond and his family, this time with direct support from the Papacy and Spain, including landings by Italian and Spanish troops in Kerry in 1579 and 1580.

1580   Revolt of Viscount Baltinglas, who leads an unsuccessful rising of Anglo-Irish Catholic gentry in Leinster.

1584   Execution of Catholic primate, Archbishop Dermot O'Hurley of Armagh (June 19), marking an intensification of the Counter-Reformation struggle in Europe, and of Queen Elizabeth's policy of religious uniformity.

1585   Composition of Connaught. Irish lords and chiefs confirmed in estates granted under English laws in return for which they surrender the rights, dues and services which they hold under Gaelic laws. The province of Connaught is thus integrated into the English system of government in Ireland.

1586   Plantation in Munster (to 1592). Efforts to establish English settlements in Munster through grants of estates to "adventurers" who agreed to colonize them. Project collapses due to massive resistance by Gaelic population.

1588   Defeat of the Spanish Armada. Many ships wrecked on the Irish coasts. All but a handful of the survivors are captured or killed.

1592   Foundation of Trinity College, Dublin, the first, and for centuries the only, institution of higher learning in Ireland. Admission is limited to adherents of the Church of Ireland.

1595   Hugh O'Neill, Earl of Tyrone, raises a rebellion in Ulster, seeking to preserve his independent rule and the Gaelic way of life against English incursions.

1598   Battle of the Yellow Ford (August). English army routed by O'Neill's forces.

O'Neill acquires support from other parts of Ireland, and, eventually, a promise of Spanish aid, though Spanish troops do not actually land in Ireland until 1601.

1601   Battle of Kinsale (December). The Irish rebels and their Spanish allies are defeated by the English.

1603   Death of Elizabeth I and accession of James I (March 24).

Surrender of the Earl of Tyrone and the remaining Irish rebels (March 30). English law is henceforth supreme throughout the four provinces of the Kingdom.

1607   Flight of the earls (September 14). The Earls of Tyrone and Tyrconnell, with many lesser lords, quit Ulster for Spain in the hope of enlisting fresh Spanish support and regaining their lost mastery in the province. This episode traditionally marks the final downfall of the old, Gaelic order in Ireland.

1608   Plantation of Ulster. Confiscated lands of the Ulster chieftans and "rebel" nobles are "planted" with English and Scottish settlers.

1633   Thomas, Viscount Wentworth (later Earl of Strafford) named Lord Deputy of Ireland, (to 1640). His heavy-handed efforts to establish the absolute authority of the Crown alienate all elements of the population.

1641   Rebellion in Ulster (October 23). Native Irish population rises against the colonists and gains control of most of the province.

1642   The Irish rebels, under the guidance of the Catholic bishops, establish a "government" at Kilkenny, comprising a Supreme Council for carrying on the war, and a "general assembly for the kingdom of Ireland." This Confederation of Kilkenny expresses alliegiance to Charles I (newly confronted by a civil war in England), provided he makes concessions to the Catholics.

1643-6   Fruitless negotiations for an alliance between the Confederates and the King. During this period, separate royal, rebel, parliamentary and Scottish armies maneuver and clash in Ireland.

1649   Campaign of Oliver Cromwell in Ireland, marked by massacres of the Irish at Drogheda (September) and Wexford (October).

Following the execution of Charles I (January), the Confederates come to terms with his successor, but are now included in the general downfall of the royalist forces.

1652   Victory of English Parliamentary forces is followed by the "Cromwellian Confiscation". Wholesale dispossession of "disaffected" landowners in favor of English settlers, largely veterans of the Cromwellian army.

1660   Restoration of the monarchy. Attempts by Charles II to carry out a land settlement (1660-5). Some dispossessed royalists reinstated in their property, but all factions are left dissatisfied by the imperfect compromise which results.

1663   Exclusion of Irish cattle from English markets. Beginning of a series of Navigation Acts and other commercial legislation aimed at subordinating the Irish economy to English interests.

1681   Execution of the Catholic primate, Archbishop Oliver Plunkett of Armagh (July 1). A by-product of the anti-Catholic uproar in England created by the "Popish Plot", this execution re-emphasized the precarious situation of the Irish Catholics, who were "tacitly tolerated" but not legally protected in their religion.

1687   Richard Talbot, Earl of Tyrconnell, named Lord Deputy (February). Appointed by the new Catholic king James II, he favors the interests of the Irish Catholics and builds up a large military force almost entirely Catholic in composition and leadership. Irish and English Protestants become fearful of coercion by "the armed might of a Catholic tyrant."

1688   "Glorious Revolution" in England, James II flees to France. Tyrconnell holds Ireland for James, except for Londonderry and a few other Protestant outposts.

1689   James II arrives in Ireland (March). Siege of Londonderry by James' army (April 19 - July 28); the Protestant population proclaims "No surrender'." and holds out for William of Orange. James summons a parliament in Dublin -- the "Patriot Parliament" (May - July).

1690 William of Orange defeats the Jacobite army at the Battle of the Boyne (July 1). James II withdraws to France, but the Jacobites continue the struggle in Ireland.

1691 Williamites defeat Jacobites at the Battle of Aughrim (July 12). Surviving Jacobite forces are besieged at Limerick (September - October).

Treaty of Limerick (October 3), whereby the Jacobite forces are allowed free passage to France, and their co-religionists left behind are promised security in property, civil rights, and exercise of their faith.

1692 Catholics excluded from the Irish Parliament. Jacobite lands confiscated and assigned to Williamites. Treaty of Limerick repudiated.

1693 Beginning of penal legislation against Catholics. They are gradually deprived of all civil rights, and retain only the most minimal rights of property and religious observance.

1699 Restrictions imposed on export of Irish woolens; continuation of English policy of curbing the growth of Irish industry during the following century stimulated the growth of a "Protestant Nationalism" among those Irishmen who possessed political rights.

1704 Test Act imposes restrictions on Protestant dissenters. Although less onerous than the Penal laws, the deprivation of full civic rights stimulated resentment among the Presbyterians of Ulster and helped motivate a large-scale emigration to America during the next seventy years.

1719 Declaratory Act of the British Parliament reasserts that body's authority "to make laws and statutes of sufficient force and validity to bind the kingdom and people of Ireland."

1724   Jonathan Swift's <u>Drapier's Letters</u> attack English policy in
              Ireland, and deny that "the people of Ireland are in some
              sort of slavery or dependence different from those of Eng-
              land."

1740-1   Famine in Ireland, resulting from the failure of the potato
              crop, upon which the mass of the population depended for
              food. This harvest blight, which caused the death of as
              many as 200,000 people, was the worst of several during
              the eighteenth century, and foreshadowed the catastrophic
              crop failures of the 1840's.

1759   Henry Flood enters Irish Parliament. He assumes leader-
              ship of the "patriot party", which has grown among Irish
              Protestants in opposition to England's political and econo-
              mic exploitation of Ireland.

1761   Beginning of Whiteboy disturbances. The "Whiteboys" a
              peasant secret society formed to resist the exactions of
              tax collectors and tithe gatherers, as well as oppressive
              landlords, carries on a guerrilla warfare of beatings,
              burnings and sabotage in the province of Munster during
              the next decade. Under a variety of names and in other
              parts of the country, but with the same basic motivation,
              such organizations continue to operate periodically down
              through the end of the century.

1767-72   George, Viscount Townshend, Lord Lieutenant of Ireland.
              In his attempts to assert the authority of the Crown against
              the entrenched "spoils system" of the Irish magnates,
              Townshend stimulates intense political activity in Ireland,
              particularly among Flood's "patriots."

1775   Henry Grattan enters Parliament, and soon supersedes
              Flood, who has abandoned the struggle, as leader of the
              "patriot party."

              War of Independence begins in America, and is followed
              with sympathetic interest in Ireland.

1778   Irish Volunteers instituted to aid in defence of the King-
              dom after the bulk of the regular garrison has been sent
              to America.

"Gardiner's Act" for relief of Catholic disabilities. This, and a second act, sponsored by Luke Gardiner, M.P., in 1782, eased certain of the restrictions on Catholics, particularly in the area of property rights, while leaving the main civil disabilities untouched.

1779   Removal of restriction on Irish trade, forced upon the British Government by a conjunction between the political power of the "patriots" and the military power of the Volunteers, who had turned their energies to the support of "Ireland's Rights."

1780   Demand for legislative autonomy raised by Grattan. His proposal that Britain recognize the exclusive right of the Irish parliament to legislate for Ireland is rejected by a pro-Government majority in the legislature.

1781   Further attempts made by Grattan and the "patriots" to overturn Poynings' Law defeated in the Irish Parliament. Thwarted in the legislature, the opposition again seeks the support of the Volunteers.

Collapse of British campaign in America (Yorktown, October) precipitates crisis in British politics and leads to fall of Lord North's Ministry.

1782   Convention of the Volunteers at Dungannon (February). They approve Grattan's assertion of Ireland's legislative autonomy and imply that they will use force to redress their grievances.

Lord Rockingham succeeeds Lord North as Prime Minister (March), and expresses sympathy with Grattan's demands. Legislative autonomy conceded by Britain (April-May). Declaratory Act repealed, Irish courts made independent.

1783   Convention of the Volunteers in Dublin (November 10). Their demands for reform of the parliamentary representation are rejected, but moderate leaders prevail upon them to disperse without a recourse to arms. The Volunteers rapidly decline in numbers and political potency after this confrontation.

1788   Regency Crisis (November). George III becomes men-
              tally deranged. The Prince of Wales seeks the Regency
              and is supported by the English Whigs and their Irish
              allies, led by Grattan. Prime Minister Pitt seeks to
              avoid a Regency, knowing that the Prince would turn him
              out. Grattan seeks to assert Irish autonomy by having
              the Dublin Parliament proclaim the Regency on its own
              initiative, regardless of what England does.

1789   The prospect of the breach between the two countries
              over the Regency is averted when George III recovers and
              resumes his duties (February).

              Outbreak of Revolution in France (July). The progress
              of the Revolution is followed with keen interest in Ireland,
              where strong sympathy for the new regime is manifested
              by reform groups.

1791   Society of United Irishmen formed in Belfast (October 14),
              and in Dublin (November 19). The organization, dedi-
              cated to the union of Irishmen of all faiths in pursuit of
              democratic reforms, is at first open and legal, but under
              the guidance of Theobald Wolfe Tone, it becomes increas-
              ingly radical and sympathetic to the idea of a republican
              revolution, on the French model.

1793   Outbreak of war between Britain and France (February
              1).

              Government-sponsored Catholic Relief Act, stimulated
              by British desire to conciliate the Catholic powers on the
              Continent. Catholics having the necessary property
              qualifications obtain the right to vote and to hold cer-
              tain civil and military offices. (March.)

1794   Suppression of United Irish Society (May 4). The move-
              ment goes underground, and its leaders soon open rela-
              tions with the revolutionary regime in France, aiming at
              an armed uprising and the establishment of an Irish Re-
              public.

1795   Earl Fitzwilliam, the newly-appointed Lord Lieutenant,
              seeks to reform the Irish Administration, but is forced
              out by the entrenched office-holders. (January-March).

This defeat marks the collapse of the moderate reform movement, inspired by Grattan. Many Irishmen now turn to the radical republicanism of the United Irish Society. Orange Order founded by Ulster Protestants after battle with members of the Catholic "Defenders" society (the "Battle of the Diamond," September 21); it aims at the maintenance of the Protestant Ascendancy and expands rapidly during the late 1790's.

1796   Tone, after a brief exile in America, arrives in France (February 1), and solicits French aid for a revolution in Ireland.

Insurrection Act passed by Irish Parliament, giving Government wide powers to curb subversion. Yeomanry units formed by "loyal" inhabitants to serve as a military police force. French invasion fleet, with Tone as passenger, reaches Bantry Bay on southern coast of Ireland, but is prevented from landing troops by prolonged and violent storms (December 22-27).

1797   "Disarming" of Ulster carried out by troops and yeomanry. Despite the brutality of their methods of search and interrogation, many arms caches remain undiscovered.

Grattan, despairing of reform, and indignant over the Government's methods, retires from Parliament.

1798   Leaders of the United Irishmen are discovered and arrested (March 12). Lord Edward Fitzgerald, the military organizer of the United Irishmen, after eluding capture for two months, is fatally wounded resisting arrest (May 19). Insurrection breaks out in Leinster (May 23) and soon spreads to Ulster. Despite initial successes, the rebels are everywhere defeated by the end of June.

Landing of a French invasion force under General Humbert and new insurrection in Connaught (August - September) come too late to revive the rebellion. Another French force, with Tone on board, is intercepted off the coast of Ulster in October. Tone, captured, takes his own life (November 19).

1799   Government-sponsored proposal of a legislative union between Britain and Ireland rejected in the Irish Parliament (January).

Strenuous efforts of Lord Lieutentant (Marquess Corn-
wallis) and Chief Secretary (Viscount Castlereagh) to win
a majority for the Union by appealing to fears of a new
rebellion or invasion, and by distributing favors and pro-
motions.

1800   Passage of the Act of Union by the Irish Parliament, and
subsequently by the British Parliament. Under its terms,
Ireland ceases to be a separate kingdom, with its own
parliament, and becomes, in effect, merely a region of
the British Isles, sending delegations of peers and commoners to the "Imperial Parliament" at Westminster.

1801   The United Kingdom of Great Britain and Ireland comes
into being (January 1).

1802   Treaty of Amiens brings about a brief peace between
Britain and France (March 27).

1803   Resumption of war between Britain and France (May 17).

Abortive rising in Dublin by remnants of United Irish
Society; trial and execution of its leader, Robert Emmet
(September).

1808   Irish Catholic bishops reject the "Veto Scheme," a proposal for Catholic emancipation which would have given
the Government the right of veto over appointments to
the hierarchy.

Daniel O'Connell, who has taken a leading part in the
veto controversy, begins his rise to the domination of
Catholic Ireland.

1813   Following the revival of Irish Catholic aspirations for
full political rights, a bill for the "relief of disabilities"
is introduced on their behalf at Westminster, but is rejected by the Imperial Parliament.

1815   End of war between Britain and France, and of the "War
of 1812" between Britain and the United States. Renewed
attention to domestic problems and discontents in England and Ireland. Resumption of Irish emigration to
America, growing steadily in volume over the next thirty
years.

1823   Daniel O'Connell founds the Catholic Association and be-
        gins a campaign to organize and direct Catholic strength
        towards the attainment of full civil rights.

1826   Election in Waterford. Thanks to the agitation carried on
        by O'Connell and the mobilization of Catholic voters by
        his followers, the candidate favored by the Catholic As-
        sociation is elected.

1827   Temporary suspension of Catholic agitation when George
        Canning becomes Prime Minister (April) in expectation
        that he will do something for Catholics. On Canning's
        death, (August) O'Connell resumes his activities.

1828   Election in Clare. Although O'Connell, as a Catholic, is
        ineligible to sit in Parliament, he enters the contest and
        is overwhelmingly elected. The Government, threatened
        with organized Catholic reaction if O'Connell's victory is
        ignored, capitulates and pushes through a "relief act."

1829   Catholic Emancipation. Catholics in Ireland (and else-
        where in Britain) are granted the right to sit in both
        Houses of Parliament and to hold all civil and military
        offices. O'Connell is hailed as "The Liberator". He be-
        comes the leader of an "Irish Party," or bloc in Parlia-
        ment, which presently gains the balance of power between
        the Whigs and the Tories.

1831   Government-supported. primary education introduced in
        Ireland.

1832   Passage of Parliamentary Reform measures, affecting
        representation in both Britain and Ireland. O'Connell's
        following in the House of Commons increases. He avows
        his intention to seek Repeal of the Act of Union and a
        restoration of Ireland's legislative autonomy.

1835   "Lichfield House Compact" between Daniel O'Connell
        and leaders of the Whig Ministry, whereby his party
        agrees to support the Government in return for promise
        of beneficial legislation for Ireland. Agitation for Repeal
        is suspended indefinitely.

1836   A more orderly and impartial administration of justice
        instituted by the Whig Chief Secretary, Thomas Drum-
        mond. A national police force established - the Irish Con-
        stabulary (re-designated "Royal Irish Constabulary" in
        1867).

1838   Tithe Act reduces burden of taxation. Poor Law Act regu-
              lates relief of the indigent.

1840   Feeling that the Whigs have not done enough for Ireland in
              terms of practical reforms, O'Connell seeks to exert
              pressure on them by founding the Loyal National Repeal
              Association (July).

1841   With the defeat of the Whigs and the return of the Tories
              to power in London, O'Connell definitely commits himself
              to a campaign for Repeal of the Act of Union. His elec-
              tion as Lord Mayor of Dublin, a non-political office,
              causes him to suspend agitation for the one year term
              (November to November 1842).

1842   Founding of The Nation by Thomas Davis and Charles
              Gavan Duffy. The newspaper, which publishes its first
              issue on October 15, supports O'Connell's Repeal Move-
              ment, but gradually becomes known as the organ of the
              Young Ireland movement.

1843   O'Connell organizes campaign of speeches and "monster
              meetings" to overawe the Government with the strength
              of the Repeal forces (June-October). Prime Minister Sir
              Robert Peel declares his willingness to bring on civil war
              rather than yield on repeal, and bans the climactic mass
              rally scheduled for October 8 at Clartarf. O'Connell,
              disavowing the use of violence, cancels the meeting. He
              is arrested and charged with conspiracy.

1844   O'Connell sentenced to one year in prison (May 30), but
              is released on appeal to House of Lords (September).
              The Repeal movement, however, has lost impetus, and
              is no longer formidable.

1845   Government proposes a system of non-sectarian "Queen's
              Colleges," which, unlike Trinity College, would be open
              to Catholics. O'Connell and Young Irelanders dispute ac-
              ceptance of this proposal (May-September). Death of
              Thomas Davis (September 16) removes moderating influ-
              ence in Young Ireland leadership.

              Potato crop destroyed by "blight" in a third of the country.
              (September-October).

1846   The Young Irelanders break with O'Connell when he in-
            sists they accept the principle of non-violence (July).

            Potato crop completely destroyed by blight (August-Sep-
            tember).

1847   Famine spreads throughout the country. Government re-
            sists appeals for massive relief measures. Efforts by
            private individuals and charitable organizations fail to
            halt ravages of malnutrition and disease. Fields aban-
            doned in many areas, so that, despite freedom from
            blight, this year's crop is too small to suffice.

            Death of O'Connell (May).

1848   Inspired by revolution in Paris (February) and elsewhere
            in Europe, the Young Irelanders raise the tricolor of
            Irish independence in Munster, but receive little support
            from an exhausted population (August). The leaders
            (William Smith O'Brien, Thomas F. Meagher, et al.) are
            captured, tried and exiled.

            Potato crop again destroyed by blight (July-September).

1849   Famine begins to abate after disappearance of blight, but
            the effects linger.

            Queen Victoria visits Ireland, and is well-received
            (August).

            Queen's Colleges opened to students in Cork, Galway and
            Belfast (October). These are joined in the Queen's Uni-
            versity in Ireland a year later (September 1850), and for
            the first time make higher education generally available
            in Ireland.

1850   Tenant Right League formed by Charles Gavan Duffy to
            secure reforms in the Irish land system, hitherto operat-
            ing exclusively to the benefit of the landlords. The
            League enjoyed a brief period of political power, and
            captured nearly half of Ireland's Parliamentary seats in
            the 1852 election, but later falls prey to internal disputes,
            and is dissolved in 1859.

1851   The census revealed a decline in Ireland's population
            from 8,196,597 in 1841, to 6,574,278 in 1851. This dimi-
            nution by 19.85% resulted from famine, epidemic disease,
            and massive emigration.

1858   Irish Republican Brotherhood (Fenians) founded. Its Irish
            branch was under the direction of James Stephens, its New
            York headquarters under that of John O'Mahony. The
            Fenians held that Ireland must be liberated by armed
            force, and prepared a secret military organization to
            strike at Britain. The hundreds of thousands of Famine
            refugees who had poured into America, were a prime
            source of manpower and financial support for the move-
            ment.

1861-5   American Civil War, in which tens of thousands of Irish
            emigrants participate, seen by the Fenians as a training
            period for Ireland's war of liberation, which they planned
            for 1865. The arrest of Stephens and other leaders of
            the Irish branch of the movement (September-November
            1865) disrupts this plan.

1866   American Fenians invade Canada, to "strike a blow
            against the Empire". The "Irish Republican Army",
            composed of Civil War veterans, defeats British forces
            sent against it, but withdraws under threat of U.S. inter-
            vention. (June.)

1867   Fenian rising in Munster repressed (March).

            Fenian "outrages" -- bombings and shootings -- in Eng-
            land (September-December).

1868   W. E. Gladstone, Prime Minister, commences policy of
            reform in Ireland which will characterize his political
            career down to 1894, despite resistance within his own
            Liberal Party.

1869   Church of Ireland disestablished and disendowed, ending
            the anomaly of a State Church to which only a fraction of
            the population belonged.

1870   Gladstone's first land act begins process of agrarian re-
            form in Ireland.

The Home Rule movement founded by Isaac Butt with the aim of securing internal self-government for Ireland.

1872   Secret voting introduced in Ireland by the Ballot Act.

Home Rule movement develops political strength.

1874   First major political success for the Home Rule movement: the election of 59 members professing Home Rule to the new House of Commons (February). They were joined in April 1875 by Charles Steward Parnell, who rapidly rose to leadership.

1877   Charles Stewart Parnell elected President of the Home Rule Confederation of Great Britain, replacing Isaac Butt (August 27).

1878   American Fenians endorse a policy of collaboration between the constitutional nationalists of Parnell's Home Rule group and the revolutionary nationalists of the Irish Republican Brotherhood (October). Although this "New Departure" was repudiated by the Fenian Supreme Council in Ireland, many Fenians threw their support to Home Rule, exchanging unproductive terrorism for political action.

1879   National Land League founded, under the instigation of Michael Davitt, the chief promoter of the Home Rule-Fenian collaboration (October 21). The league organized resistance to the landlords to halt evictions and secure fair rents, aiming ultimately at making the tenant farmers masters of their own land.

1880   "Land War" in Ireland between supporters of the Land League and its goals and the estate-owners and their agents. Ostracism developed as a technique of moral warfare in the case of Captain Charles Boycott, a land agent in Mayo, gives rise to the term and tactic of "boycotting."

1881   Gladstone, back in office, combines a second land act with various coercive measures in an effort to end Land War. Unsuccessful, he arrests Davitt and Parnell and outlaws the Land League (October).

1882   "Kilmainham Treaty" between Gladstone and Parnell.
            Irish leaders released from prison, Land War ended on
            compromise terms ultimately favorable to tenants.

1885   Asbourne Act establishes a system of state aid for pur-
            chase of land by the tenant occupier. Through this and
            subsequent supplementary legislation, Ireland is trans-
            formed during the next two decades from a country of
            great estates into one whose land is owned by individual
            small farmers.

1886   Gladstone introduces a home-rule bill, which will give
            Ireland its own parliament and self-government (April).
            The home-rule bill is defeated in the House of Commons
            (June) and Gladstone himself forced out of office (July).
            Revival of religious strife in Ulster, as agitators warn
            Protestants that "Home Rule means Rome Rule." Scores
            of Catholics killed and injured in Belfast rioting.

1887-9   Conflicts in Ireland over the Catholic Church's attitude
            towards Parnell and his movement.

            Uproar in England over Parnell's alleged endorsement of
            political assassination ending when the "evidence" is
            shown to be a forgery.

1890   Fall of Parnell, who is ousted from leadership of Irish
            Parliamentary party after outcry over his involvement
            in a divorce case (December).

1891   Death of Parnell (October 6), who is succeeded as leader
            of the Parliamentary faction loyal to Parnell by John Red-
            mond (December). . The Irish nationalists are divided,
            however, and can no longer exercise a pivotal role in
            British politics.

1893   Gladstone (back in office, August 1892) introduces a
            second home rule bill (February). It passes Commons,
            but is rejected in the House of Lords (September).

            The Gaelic League founded (July 31) to promote cultural
            nationalism. Its guiding spirit, Dr. Douglas Hyde, urges
            a thorough "de-Anglicization" -- a "refusal to imitate the
            English in their language, literature, music, games,
            dress and ideas."

1895   Return of Conservatives to office after general election
              (July) marks end of home rule prospects for more than a
              decade. The nationalist initiative begins to pass from
              parliamentarians to cultural and labor leaders.

1896   Foundation of the Irish Socialist Republican Party by
              James Connolly.

1898   James Connolly, Socialist labor leader, founds his news-
              paper The Workers' Republic (August).

              The Government concedes a measure of local self-govern-
              ment by the establishment of county councils in Ireland.

1899   The Gaelic Revival's progress is marked by the publica-
              tion of An Glaidheamh Soluis, the official organ of the
              Gaelic League. The development of a distinctive Anglo-
              Irish literary movement is marked by the foundation of
              the Irish Literary Theatre (later - 1902 - the Irish Na-
              tional Theatre Society).

1905   Unionist Council formed in Ulster to oppose any conces-
              sions on Home Rule. Revival of militant Protestant oppo-
              sition to nationalist movements.

1906   The Liberals return to office (February). The Irish
              Parliamentary Party, re-united, since 1900, under the
              leadership of John Redmond, seeks new opportunities to
              advance its program.

1908   Sinn Fein Party established (September). Based upon the
              political philosophy of Arthur Griffith, editor of the
              United Irishman (founded 1899) and author of The Resur-
              rection of Hungary (1904), it proposes the withdrawal of
              all Irish M.P.'s from Parliament, to form a national
              council, which would take over the government of Ireland,
              retaining only the link of a common crown with Britain --
              a "dual monarchy" similar to that which connected Hun-
              gary with Austria.

1909   Irish Transport and General Workers' Union formed by
              James Larkin and James Connolly (January).

1910   In General Elections held in February and December, the
              Irish Parliamentary Party holds the deciding balance of
              votes between the evenly-matched Conservatives and
              Liberals.

Sir Edward Carson elected Chairman of the Irish Unionist Party, pledged to resist Home Rule. (February).

1912   Liberal Government introduces third Home Rule Bill, which passes Commons, but is defeated in the Lords.

Protestant opponents of Home Rule swear, in the "Solemn League and Covenant" to defeat the Home Rule conspiracy by "all means which may be found necessary" (September).

1913   Home Rule Bill, repassed by Commons, is again defeated by the Lords (July).

Mounting tensions in Ireland between Ulster Unionists and nationalists. An Ulster Volunteer Force is formed in January, and a "Provisional Government of Ulster" formed (September) to take over administration of the province if Home Rule is passed. Two nationalist para-military forces are created during November -- the Citizen Army, based on James Connolly's labor unions and the National Volunteers, dominated by the Irish Republican Brotherhood.

1914   Home Rule Bill passes Commons for the third time (May), and can no longer be blocked by the Lords. It receives royal assent in September, but its implementation is suspended pending the end of the European War.

Redmond, leader of the Irish Party in Parliament, urges Irishmen to fight for Britain against Germany. The National Volunteers split, with many adhering to the I.R.B. plan of non-cooperation. The leadership of the I.R.B. decides on an insurrection while Britain is occupied with the war (September).

1915   Alliance between the Citizen Army and the Irish Volunteers (the I.R.B. - controlled remnant of the former National Volunteers). (November). Both para-military forces drill openly - in uniform and with arms - while British authorities refrain from interference lest they provoke violence.

1916   Insurrection in Dublin by Volunteers and Citizen Army. P. H. Pearse, Commander of the Volunteers, proclaims

the birth of the Irish Republic (April 24). After a week of
fighting in the capital, the rebels surrender, and their
leaders (Pearse, Connolly et al.) are executed (May 3-12).

Although the insurrection receives little support outside
of Dublin, the swift and brutal British reprisals against
the captured rebels arouse public opinion throughout Ireland.

1917   In the aftermath of the Rising, Sinn Fein emerges as a
              powerful political force, and Eamon De Valera, a surviv-
              ing leader of the Rising, is elected to Parliament as a
              Sinn Fein candidate in East Clare (July).

1918   European War ends (November). General Election in
              Ireland (December). Sinn Fein wins 73 seats in the
              House of Commons to 26 for the Ulster Unionists and only
              6 for Redmond's party.

1919   The Sinn Fein M.P.'s, following Griffith's program, ignore
              the Westminster Parliament, and constitute themselves
              an Irish National Assembly -- Dail Eireann. They re-
              assert the existence of the Irish Republic with a declara-
              tion of independence and a provisional constitution (Janu-
              ary 21). De Valera elected President of the Dail (April 1).
              As head of the republican government, he is assisted by
              Griffith, who directs "home affairs" and Michael Collins
              of the Volunteers, who organizes the Irish Republican
              Army (IRA). Outbreak of the Anglo-Irish War ("the
              Troubles").

1920   Guerrilla warfare between IRA and British troops, rein-
              forced by two special constabulary units, the Auxiliaries,
              and the "Black and Tans." Terrorism and counter-terror-
              ism, assassination and reprisal continue throughout the
              year.

              British government attempts to end the war by offering
              Home Rule separately to the Dail and to the Orange lead-
              ers in Belfast. The Ulster Unionists now accept Home
              Rule for their own region. Under the Government of Ire-
              land Act, Northern Ireland (Antrim, Down, Arnagh, Lon-
              donderry, Fermanagh, Tyrone) acquires its own Parlia-
              ment and regional administration.

1921 King George V presides at the opening session of the Parliament of Northern Ireland (June 22) and pleads for peace throughout Ireland.

  Truce declared between Britain and the Dail (July 11). Griffith and Collins open negotiations in London. Anglo-Irish treaty signed (December 6), confirming peace on the basis of dominion status for southern Ireland (the remaining 26 counties).

1922 Anglo-Irish treaty ratified by Dail by a 64-57 vote, with De Valera and his supporters opposing dominion status as a betrayal of Ireland's right to complete independence as a sovereign republic (January 7).

  Irish Free State established. Griffith elected President of the Dail; Collins head of the provisional government. General election for a new Dail returns a majority of pro-treaty representatives (June).

  British troops withdraw from Ireland; facilities and equipment handed over to the new army of the Irish Free State.

  De Valera and the republicans launch a civil war against the Free State (June).

  Battle in Dublin between Free State and Republican forces (July).

  Death of Arthur Griffith (August 12). Death of Michael Collins, killed in an ambush by republicans (August 22).

  William T. Cosgrave becomes President of the Executive Council (i.e., head of the Free State government).

1923 Republicans lay down their arms, ending civil war (April).

  Irish Free State enters League of Nations.

1925 Boundary Commission fails to establish basis for revision of Six-County frontier. Partition of Ireland continues.

  Breach between De Valera and IRA over future relationship of republicans with the Free State.

1927　　De Valera re-enters politics. His party, the Fianna Fail, participates in the General Election, and becomes the largest opposition group in the Dail.

1929　　IRA establishes political party, Saor Eire, to further republican and anti-partition goals.

1930　　Irish Free State elected to the Council of the League of Nations.

1931　　Statute of Westminster defines relationship of dominions to the Commonwealth and to Britain (December). Irish delegates played a significant role in producing this statute.

Public Safety Act, initiated by Free State Government, restrains political activity of Saor Eire, the IRA's party.

1932　　Fianna Fail wins General Election; De Valera becomes head of government, a post he will hold until 1948.

Start of "Economic War" with Britain, when De Valera withholds the £5 million annual annuities payment due on the small farmers' purchase of land from British estate owners. Britain retaliates by taxing the import of Irish cattle into Britain. De Valera, in turn, imposes new customs duties on British imports. Despite the damage already done to Ireland by the worldwide "depression," the economic war will continue for six years.

De Valera elected President of the League Council.

1936　　After an outbreak of political violence and assassination, De Valera bans the IRA and imprisons its leaders.

Irish contingents fight as volunteers in both sides in the Spanish Civil War, IRA detachments supporting the Republic, members of the Army Comrades' Association ("Blue Shirts") aiding the Nationalists.

1937　　Following the abdication of Edward VIII (December 1936) the External Relations Act terminates the Free State's relationship to the British Crown.

New Constitution adopted by vote of the Dail (June 14).
The Irish Free State formally changes its name to Eire,
"a sovereign, independent and democratic state." Although Eire no longer participated in Commonwealth Con-
ferences after 1937, the designation of "republic" was
not specifically chosen for the new state, and the British
monarch continued to be recognized as "an instrument
for validating the accreditation" of Irish diplomats.

1938   Douglas Hyde becomes first President of Eire (January).

Anglo-Irish pact ends economic war on the basis of a
final lump sum annuity payment of Ł10 million. In addition, Britain agrees to evacuate the three naval bases in
Ireland which had been left at her disposal by the 1922
treaty (April 25).

1939   Outbreak of Second World War (September). Premier
De Valera declares that Eire cannot support Britain in
the war while Ireland, denied national self-determination, remains partitioned. He proclaims Ireland's neutrality in the war.

Revival of IRA activity in England; many bomb incidents,
notably at Coventry (August 25), in which 75 persons are
killed or wounded. After the execution and imprisonment
of many IRA men during 1940, and the failure of promised
German aid, the organization languishes during the re-
mainder of the war.

1940   Eire resists pressure from Britain to allow use of naval
and air bases vital to the protection of Atlantic shipping.

Armed forces of Eire increased and placed on alert to
resist possible invasion by Britain or Germany.

1941   Belfast bombed by German planes (April 15-16). Eire
sends fire-fighting units across the border to assist
the Northern fire-brigades.

Strong pressure from U.S. Government on De Valera to
make air and naval bases available for anti-submarine
patrol. Although these urgings are redoubled after the
U.S. enters the war (December), De Valera insists on
maintaining neutrality.

1942   De Valera protests stationing of American troops in Nor-
        thern Ireland.

        Despite Eire's neutrality, some thirty thousand of her
        citizens enlist in the British armed forces. In the Six
        Counties, where the London Government, heeding De-
        Valera's admonition, did not impose conscription, thou-
        sands more volunteer.

1945   End of Second World War. Prime Minister Churchill's
        victory speech includes a denunciation of Ireland's neu-
        trality (May 13). De Valera's reply (May 16) is a re-
        assertion of his policy and a re-dedication to the principle
        of a united Ireland.

        Sean T. O'Kelly succeeds Douglas Hyde as President of
        Eire.

1946   Ireland's application for membership in the United Na-
        tions is blocked by the Soviet Union.

1948   General election. Fianna Fail loses its majority in the
        Dail, and De Valera is superseded by John A. Costello,
        at the head of an "inter-party" administration.

        External Relations Act of 1936 repealed, formally end-
        ing Eire's ties with the Commonwealth and her recogni-
        tion of the British monarch's role in accrediting diplomats
        (December 21).

1949   Irish Government rejects invitation to participate in North
        Atlantic Treaty Organization as long as Britain maintains
        partition. (February 8).

        The Republic of Ireland formally proclaimed (April 18).

1951   Resignation of Costello Government after dispute among
        members of Coalition Cabinet. De Valera again becomes
        Premier (June 13).

1953   After Fianna Fail has lost several by-elections, DeValera
        seeks and wins a vote of confidence in the Dail (July 2).

1954   De Valera's Government, after maintaining itself precari-
        ously for three years, despite a minority of seats in the

Dail, is brought down by a new combination of opposition
parties. John A. Costello heads a new "inter-party" administration.

1955   Ireland is admitted to the United Nations (December 14).

Government's program of heavy capital investment to
develop national industry and resources leads to fiscal
problems.

1956   IRA begins a series of raids and bombings along the Six
County frontier (to 1962).

Economic crisis; balance of payments deficit. Government imposes fiscal restraints which retard growth rate,
precipitate increased unemployment and emigration.

1957   Fall of Costello Government. DeValera again Premier.
Efforts by Sean Lemass, Minister for Trade and Commerce, to develop a scheme of economic recovery.

1958   Government undertakes program of economic expansion,
involving great increase in capital investment, solicita-
tion of foreign investment, industrial development, promotion of tourism, etc.

Ireland contributes 50 army officers to U.N. Observer
Corps in the Middle East.

1959   Eamon DeValera succeeds Sean T. O'Kelly as President
of the Republic. Sean Lemass becomes Premier (June
23).

1960   Irish troops dispatched to Congo to serve with U.N. forces; Lt. General McKeown of the Irish Army eventually
becomes commander of all U.N. troops there.

Ambassador Frederick Boland of Ireland elected President of the U.N. General Assembly.

1961   Irish application for admission to the European Economic
Community (July).

Irish participation in U.N.E.S.C.O. (October).

1963   Completion of first program of economic expansion,
            which had quadrupled the annual economic growth rate in
            five years, with a 75% increase in the gross national pro-
            duct and a doubling of investment. A second program,
            for 1964-1970, is projected.

1964   Ireland dispatches troops to assist U.N. peace-keeping
            force in Cyprus.

1965   Lemass and Terence O'Neill, Prime Minister of Northern
            Ireland, exchange visits to each other's capitals (January-
            February), inaugurating a new stage in friendly relations
            and discussion of mutual problems between the two Irish
            Governments.

1966   Ratification of Anglo-Irish trade agreement (January).

            Resignation of Sean Lemass, who is succeeded as Prem-
            ier by John Lynch, Minister of Finance. (November 10).

            Premier Lynch and Prime Minister Harold Wilson meet
            in London to negotiate a common approach to the Euro-
            pean Economic Community (December).

1967   Northern Ireland Civil Rights Association founded (Febru-
            ary 6), to seek equality in employment, housing, fran-
            chise, etc. for Catholics in the Six Counties.

1968   Catholic civil rights demonstrations in Northern Ireland.

            Clash between demonstrators and Royal Ulster Constabu-
            lary in Londonderry (October 5).

1969   Civil Rights groups stage march from Belfast to London-
            derry, and are attacked by Unionist mobs enroute. (Janu-
            ary).

            Rioting between Catholics and Protestants in Belfast and
            Londonderry. British troop reinforcements sent to
            Northern Ireland to "maintain order." (August).

            Split in IRA between Official (Marxist) wing and Provi-
            sional (Nationalistic) wing.

1970   Attacks on British troops in Belfast by IRA. Curfews im-
                posed on Catholic areas of the city.

1971   Northern Ireland Government orders the internment of
                suspected IRA "activists" (August).

1972   British troops fire on a Catholic crowd in Belfast, killing
                13 and wounding 17 (January 30). Demonstrations, pro-
                testing the "Bloody Sunday" shooting held on both sides of
                the border (February). British Government removes the
                Northern Ireland Administration, suspends the local Par-
                liament, and imposes direct rule (March 24). Ireland
                and Britain admitted to European Economic Community
                (April).

                "Official" IRA agrees to ceasefire in Northern Ireland in
                response to conciliatory gestures from British authori-
                ties; "Provisional" IRA continues its use of force (May).

                William Whitelaw, Secretary of State for Northern Ire-
                land, seeks to calm Protestant fears that Britain will
                abandon Northern Ireland, following a week of Protestant
                demonstrations and marches by militant groups, such as
                the "Ulster Vanguard." He announces that more troops
                are being brought into the province, and rejects a cease-
                fire offer (linked with direct negotiations) from the Pro-
                visional IRA, declaring that he "cannot respond to ulti-
                matums from terrorists." (June 12-13).

                The Dublin Government, having arrested a number of
                leading IRA officers in the South, establishes "special
                criminal courts" to try them, in the Republic's first
                major effort to control the illegal organizations' activi-
                ties within her border (May-June).

POYNINGS' LAW, 1494

Source: <u>Statutes at Large Passed in the Parliaments Held in Ireland, 1310-1800</u>. (Dublin, 1786-1801), I, 44.

An act that no parliament be holden in this land
until the acts be certified into England.

Item, at the request of the commons of the land of Ireland, be it ordained, enacted and established, that at the next parliament that there shall be holden by the king's commandment and licence, wherein amongst other the king's grace intendeth to have a general resumption of his whole revenues since the last day of the reign of King Edward the second, no parliament be holden hereafter in the said land, but at such season as the king's lieutenant and council there first do certify the king, under the great seal of that land, the causes and considerations, and all such acts as then seemeth should pass in the same parliament, and such causes, considerations, and acts affirmed by the king and his council to be good and expedient for that land, and his licence thereupon, as well in affirmation of the said causes and acts, as to summon the said parliament, under his great seal of England had and obtained; that done, a parliament to be hand and holden after the form and effect afore rehearsed: and if any parliament be holden in that land hereafter, contrary to the form and provision aforesaid, it be deemed void and of none effect in law.

A DEPUTY'S INSTRUCTIONS, 1530

Source: State Papers During the Reign of Henry VIII (London, Lemon, 1830-
         52), II, 147-50.

Instructions, given by the king's highness to his trusty councillor, Sir
William Skeffington, knight, master of the ordnance, whom his grace hath
constituted and ordained to be deputy unto his right trusty and right entirely
well-beloved cousin, the Duke of Richmond and of Somerset, lieutenant of
his land of Ireland, as followeth.

First, the said Sir William Skeffington, taking with him the king's
letters credentials directed to the chancellor, and other the king's coun-
cillors, of his said land of Ireland, shall at his repair thither, assemble
them together, delivering unto them the king's said letters and showing
unto them the cause of his coming and repair thither at this time; which is,
to serve the king's highness in the office and room aforesaid, according
to the effect of the letters patent made unto him upon the same, which the
said deputy shall there exhibit and show, taking thereupon his admission to
the same room, in such manner as in that case is accustomed. Which done,
the said deputy shall consult, common, and devise with the said council,
at good length and deliberation, upon all such points and matters, as by
them shall be thought good now to proceed unto, for the surety, weal, and
defense of that land; so as, by their discreet and politic orders and endeavours, the same may be preserved in as good tranquility, obedience,
order of justice, and quiet, as may be, the king's lands there well defended,
and the king's rebellious subjects of the wild Irishry resisted in their attempts and invasions, the best they can. For the better accomplishment
whereof, the king's highness sendeth now with the said deputy, for his more
strength and assistance, not only the number of 200 horsemen, there to
reside and demur upon the tuition and defense of the king's said land and
good subjects of the same, but also money for contentation and payment of
their wages; whom, the king's trust is, the said deputy will employ to such
good purpose, as may surely serve to the defence aforesaid; whereunto
nothing shall more confer, than to conserve and keep the king's said good
subjects in good unity, love and concord, repressing and reforming all
particular grudges and displeasures, which be, or may grow, among any
of them, and chiefly and principally, between the king's right well-beloved
cousins, the earls of Kildare, Desmond, and Ossory, who be the persons
most able there, with their powers and assistance effectually (from time to
time) given to the said deputy, to resist the malice of the enemies and to
preserve the king's land from invasion and annoyance. And therefore the
said deputy, with the rest of the said council, must have special regard
thereunto, so that all rancours and displeasures between the said earls,
and any of them, may be clearly removed;...

And albeit that the king's highness, minding and intending graciously
to assist the noblemen and other his good subjects, of the said land, for

their weal, surety, and defence, doth, as is aforesaid, now send the said number of persons to reside and demur, as is before mentioned; yet, nevertheless, it is not the mind nor intention of his highness, that the said deputy, or any other, shall employ them, nor any other of the king's subjects in the said land, upon the wild Irishry at such charges of the country, as in such main hostings is used, without the express consent, knowledge and agreement of the whole council, or the more part of them; but that they intend to the sure preservation and defence of the said land, resisting the enemies with all such policies and advantages as be to be taken against them, as far as shall be thought convenient to the said deputy; not taking any such hosting, charging the country otherwise than for victual as they pass, like as in such other journies hath been accustomed. Nevertheless whensoever, and as often as it shall be fully agreed and determined with the advice and consent of the whole council of the said land, or the more part of them, for any great cause or benefit, to make a hosting and main invasion, charging the country for exploits to be done against the enemies, the said Sir William Skeffington shall now, in that case, else not, use and employ, his said number to that purpose, as by the said council shall be agreed and thought expedient, and otherwise in no manner, either with them or without, make any such host, at the charge of the country, but by the advice of the council, or the most part of them, otherwise than is aforesaid.

The said deputy shall also take with him the letters patent, under the king's seal of Ireland, devised upon all such articles and points, as there were thought good to be enacted and passed by authority of the parliament of his said land; which parliament the said deputy shall call and convoke with as good diligence as he shall see to be necessary and requisite, endeavouring him, with the assistance of the residue of the said council, to the establishment, enacting, and passing of such acts, by the authority aforesaid, as by the king's highness shall be devised, and to the due certificate to be made unto the king's highness thereof, as is accustomed, and semblably to the execution and performance of the same, after such sort and manner, as may be to the weal of the king's said people and land, and after such form as the said articles do purport. The discreet ordering whereof, for attaining them to pass, the king's highness committeth to the wisdom and endeavour of the said deputy, with the assistance of the residue of the council as is aforesaid.

Among other things to be treated and communed of at the assembly of the said council, upon the first arrival in Ireland of the said deputy, it is specially to be remembered, that he, with the same council, devise and consult together for the immediate conducing and attaining of a subsidy within the said land, towards the supportation and alleviation of the king's charges; endeavouring them, to the best of their powers, to have the same subsidy payable for one year to be ended at Michaelmas next, and that failing, for half a year ending the same day, if they can so conduce it, and also to induce for as many years as they can attain the same. Which thing is not to be tracted or retracted till the parliament, forasmuch as perchance the same shall not be assembled till Michaelmas next, but is, with all convenient diligence, to be practised and brought to pass before the said parliament, if it may be, as both the said deputy, and also the council aforesaid, can and do well consider. And the sums rising out of the same subsidy, and of all other the king's revenues and profits in that land, the said deputy shall cause and suffer to be answered and payed to the hands of the prior of Kilmainham, under-treasurer there, without intermeddling or taking any part thereof to himself, but to see the king duly answered thereof, as to reason doth appertain.

And whereas the earl of Kildare hath made faithful promise unto the king's highness to employ and endeavour himself, to the uttermost of his power, for the annoyance of the king's said rebellious subjects of the wild Irishry, as well by making excourses upon them, as otherwise; forasmuch as the men of war, now sent out of this realm with the said deputy, shall now, in such case, do right good stead to the said earl, in such exploits as he shall make, when the said deputy shall not fortune to proceed thereunto himself (he) shall, at the requisition of the said earl, send unto him the said men of war, or as many of them as he shall require for making of such exploits, reserving a convenient number of them to remain and attend upon himself; and the profits of such impositions, that is to say, of beasts, or other things, that at an entry or exploit shall be imponed or had by way of patisement or agreement, upon the enemies, to be always the half answered to the king's highness, to the hands of the said under-treasurer, and the other half to render to the earl of Kildare, if he shall make the exploits and put the imposition, and to his company not having the king's wages, to be ordered and divided by his discretion, as hath been accustomed.

Finally, the said deputy shall from time to time as well by his letters apart, as also jointly with the residue of the king's said council, advertise the king's highness of the state and successes of the affairs in the said land of Ireland; endeavouring himself always with diligence to those things, which by common advice of the said council, shall be thought good, both for administration of justice, punishment of transgressors and malefactors, good order, quiet, the farms, wards, marriages, and other the king's profits there, aforesaid, and also for the resistance of the malice and temerity of the king's said rebellious subjects; using all politic provisions, as well as by appointments to be taken with them, when the case shall require, as by force and other good and discreet ways as shall be thought convenient; and, generally, shall do, observe, and accomplish all such things, as to the office, authority, and trust, which the king's highness, of special confidence, hath and doth put him in, shall appertain; whereby he shall more and more deserve the king's special favour and thanks, to be hereafter remembered to his weal accordingly.

HENRY VIII PROCLAIMED KING OF IRELAND, 1541

Source: Statutes at Large Passed in the Parliaments Held in Ireland 1310-
1800 (Dublin, 1786-1801), I, 176-7.

An act that the king of England, his heirs and his
successors be kings of Ireland.

Forasmuch as the king our most gracious dread sovereign lord, and his grace's most noble progenitors, kings of England, have been lords of this land of Ireland, having all manner kingly jurisdiction, power, pre-eminence, and authority royal, belonging or appertaining to the royal estate and majesty of a king, by the name of lords of Ireland. where the king's ma esty and his noble progenitors, justly and rightfully were. and of right ought to be kings of Ireland, and so to be reputed. taken, named and called, and for lack of naming the king's ma esty and his noble progenitors kings of Ireland, according to their said true and just title. style and name therein, hath been great occasion that the Irish men and inhabitants within this realm of Ireland have not been so obedient to the king's highness and his most noble progenitors, and to their laws, as they of right, and according to their allegiance and bounden duties ought to have been. Wherefore, at the humble pursuit, petition, and request of the lords spiritual and temporal, and other the king's loving, faithful and obedient subjects of this his land of Ireland and by their full assents. be it enacted, ordained, and established by authority of this present parliament, that the king's highness, his heirs and successors, kings of England be always kings of this land of Ireland, and that his majesty, his heirs and successors have the name. style, title, and honour of king of this land of Ireland, with all manner honours, pre-eminence, prerogatives, dignities, and other things whatsoever they be, to the estate and majesty of a king imperial appertaining or belonging; and that his majesty, his heirs and successors, be from henceforth named, called, accepted, reputed, and taken to be kings of this land of Ireland, to have, hold, and enjoy the said style, title. maiesty, and honours of king of Ireland, with all manner pre-eminences, prerogatives, dignities and all other the premises, unto the king's highness, his heirs and successors for ever, as united and knit to the imperial crown of the realm of England.

II. And be it further enacted by authority aforesaid, that on this side the first day of July next coming, proclamation shall be made in all shires within this land of Ireland, of the tenor and sentences of this act. And if any person or persons, of what estate, dignity, or condition soever they or he be, subject or resident within this land of Ireland, after the said first day of July, by writing or imprinting, or by any exterior act or deed, maliciously procure or do, or cause to be procured or done, any thing or things to the peril of the king's majesty's most royal person, or maliciously give occasion by writing, deed, print, or act, whereby the king's majesty,

his heirs or successors, or any of them might be disturbed or interrupted
of the crown of this realm of Ireland, or of the name, style, or title thereof, or by writing, deed, print, or act procure or do, or cause to be procured or done, any thing or things, to the prejudice, slander, disturbance,
or derogation of the king's majesty, his heirs or successors, in, of or for
the crown of this realm of Ireland, or in, of or for the name, title or style
thereof, whereby his majesty, his heirs or successors, or any of them
might be disturbed or interrupted in body, name, style, or title of inheritance, of, in or to the crown of this land of Ireland, or of the name, style,
title, or dignity of the same, that then every such person and persons, of
what estate, degree or condition they be, subject or residents within the
said land of Ireland, and their aiders, counsellors, maintainers, and abet-
tors therein, and every of them, for every such offense, shall be adjudged
high traitors, and ... shall suffer pains of death, as in cases of high treason; and also shall lose and forfeit unto the king's highness, and to his heirs,
kings of this realm of Ireland, all such his manors, lands, tenements, rents,
reversions, annuities, and hereditaments, which they had in possession
as owner, and were sole seised in their own right, or, by, or in any title
or means. . .

THE EARL OF TYRONE'S NON-NEGOTIABLE DEMANDS, 1599

Source: <u>Calendar of State Papers relating to Ireland</u>, 1599-1600 (London, 1899), pp. 279-81.

Articles intended to be stood upon by Tyrone.

1.   That the catholic, apostolic, and Roman religion be openly preached and taught throughout all Ireland, as well in cities as borough towns, by bishops, seminary priests, jesuits, and all other religious men.

2.   That the Church of Ireland be wholly governed by the pope.

3.   That all cathedrals and parish churches, abbeys, and all other religious houses, with all tithes and church lands, now in the hands of the English, be presently restored to the catholic churchmen.

4.   That all Irish priests and religious men, now prisoners in England or Ireland, be presently set at liberty, with all temporal Irishmen, that are troubled for their conscience, and to go where they will, without further trouble.

5.   That all Irish priests and religious men may freely pass and re-pass, by sea and land, to and from foreign countries.

6.   That no Englishman may be a churchman in Ireland.

7.   That there be erected an university upon the crown rents of Ireland, wherein all sciences shall be taught according to the manner of the catholic Roman church.

8.   That the governor of Ireland be at least an earl, and of the privy council of England, bearing the name of viceroy.

9.   That the lord chancellor, lord treasurer, lord admiral, the council of state, the justices of the laws, queen's attorney, queen's serjeant, and all other officers appertaining to the council and law of Ireland, be Irishmen.

10.   That all principal governments of Ireland, as Connaught, Munster, etc., be governed by Irish noblemen.

11.   That the master of ordnance, and half the soldiers with their officers resident in Ireland, be Irishmen.

12.   That no Irishman's heirs shall lose their lands for the faults of their ancestors.

13.   That no Irishman's heir under age shall fall in the queen's or her successors' hands, as a ward, but that the living be put to the heir's profit, and the advancement of his younger brethren, and marriages of his sisters, if he have any.

14.   That no children nor any other friends be taken as pledges for the good abearing of their parents, and, if there be any such pledges now in the hands of the English, they must presently be released.

15.   That all statutes made against the preferment of Irishmen as well in their own country as abroad, be presently recalled.

16.   That the queen nor her successors may in no sort press an Irish-

man to serve them against his will.

17.   That O'Neill, O'Donnell, the Earl of Desmond, with all their par-
takers may peacable enjoy all lands and privileges that did appertain to
their predecessors 200 years past.

18.   That all Irishmen, of what quality they be, may freely travel in
foreign countries, for their better experience, without making any of the
queen's officers acquainted withal.

19.   That all Irishmen may freely travel and traffic all merchandise
in England as Englishmen, paying the same rights and tributes as the English do.

20.   That all Irishmen may freely traffic with all merchandises, that
shall be thought necessary by the council of state of Ireland for the profit
of their republic, with foreigners or in foreign countries, and that no Irishman shall be troubled for the passage of priests or other religious men.

21.   That all Irishmen that will may learn, and use all occupations and
arts whatsoever.

22.   That all Irishmen may freely build ships of what burden they will,
furnishing the same with artillery and all munition at their pleasure. --
(1599, November)

GRIEVANCES OF THE REBELS, 1641

Source: E. Lodge, _Desiderata Curiosa Hibernica_, Dublin: R. Burke, 1772.

Heads of the causes which moved the Northern Irish, and
Catholicks of Ireland, to take arms (1641)

1. IT was plotted and resolved by the Puritans of England, Scotland, and Ireland, to extinguish quite the Catholick religion, and the professors and maintainers thereof, out of all those kingdoms; and to put all Catholicks of this realm to the sword, that would not conform themselves to the protestant religion.

2. THE State of Ireland did publickly declare, that they would root out of this realm all the natives, and make a total second conquest of the land, alledging, that they were not safe with them.

3. ALL the natives here were deprived of the benefit of the ancient fundamental laws, liberties, and privileges, due by all laws and justice to a free people and nation, and more particularly due by the municipal laws of Ireland.

4. THAT the subjects of Ireland, especially the Irish, were thrust out forcibly from their ancient possessions, against law, without colour or right; and could not have propriety or security in their estates, goods or other rights, but were wholly subject to an arbitrary power, and tyrannical government, these forty years past, without hope of relief or redress.

5. THEIR native youth here, debarred by the practice of state, from all learning and education, in that the one only university here, excludes all Catholicks thence; neither are they suffered to acquire learning or breeding beyond seas, of purpose to make them rude and ignorant of all letters.

6. THE Catholicks of this realm are not admitted to any dignity, place, or office, either military or civil, spiritual or temporal, but the same conferred upon unworthy persons, and men of no quality, who purchase it for money, or favour, and not by merit.

7. ALL the trading, traffick, shipping, and riches of this whole isle by the corruption of the State, are engrossed by the Dutch, Scottish, and English, not residing here, who exclude the natives wholly from the same; and who return the product, and all their flock and coin back into their native countries.

8. ALL the staple and rich commodities of the realm are turned to monopolies, and heavy impositions against law laid on all merchandize.

9. THE principal native wares of the land exported into foreign parts, unwrought and unmanufactured, thereby depriving the kingdom of all manual trades and occupations; and driving the natives to furnish themselves from head to foot, with manufacturers from abroad, at very dear rates.

10. ALL their heavy and insufferable pressures prosecuted and laboured by the natives of this kingdom, with much suit, expense, and importunity, both in parliament here, and in England before his Majesty, to

to be redressed, yet could never be brought to any happy conclusion, or as much as hope of contentment, but always eluded with delays.

11. COMMON justice, and the rights and privileges of parliament, denied to all the natives of the realm; and the ancient course of parliamentary proceeding wholly declined.

12. HIS majesty's royal power, honour, prerogative, estate, revenue, and rights, invaded upon, by the puritan faction in England. . . .

17. ALL the natives in the English plantations of this realm, were disarmed by proclamation, and the protestant plantators armed, and tied by the conditions of their plantations, to have arms, and to keep certain number of horse and foot continually upon their lands, by which advantage, many thousands of the natives were expulsed out of their possessions, and as many hanged by martial law, without cause, and against the laws of this realm; and many of them otherwise destroyed, and made away, by sinister means and practices.

18. HALF this realm was found to belong unto his majesty, as his ancient demesne and inheritance, upon old feigned titles of three hundred years past, by juries, against law, their evidence and conscience who were corrupted to find the said titles, upon promise of part of those lands so found for the king, or other reward, or else were drawn thereunto by threats of the judges in the circuits, or by heavy fines, mulcts, and censures of pillory, stigmatizings, and other like cruel and unusual punishments.

AN ACT FOR THE SPEEDY AND EFFECTUAL REDUCING OF THE REBELS
IN HIS MAJESTY'S KINGDOM OF IRELAND TO THEIR DUE OBEDIENCE TO
HIS MAJESTY AND THE CROWN OF ENGLAND, 1641.

Source: Statutes of the Realm of England (London, 1810-22), V, 168-72.

Whereas the lords and commons taking into their serious considerations as well the necessity of a speedy reducing of the rebels of Ireland to
their due obedience as also the great sums of money that the commons of
this realm have of late paid for the public and necessary affairs of this kingdom, whereof the lords and commons are very sensible, and desirous to
embrace all good and honourable ways tending to his majesty's greatness and
profit, the settling of that realm and the ease of his majesty's subjects of
England, and whereas diverse worthy and well affected persons perceiving
that many millions of acres of the rebels' lands of that kingdom which go
under the name of profitable lands, will be confiscate and to be disposed of,
and that in case two millions and an half of those acres, to be equally taken
out of the four provinces of that kingdom, may be allotted for the satisfaction
of such persons as shall disburse any sums of money for the reducing of the
rebels there, (it) would effectually accomplish the same, have made these
propositions ensuing:
  1. That two millions and a half of those acres may be assigned allotted
and divided amongst them after this proportion, viz. for each adventure of
two hundred pounds one thousand acres in Ulster, for three hundred pounds
one thousand acres in Connaught, for four hundred and fifty pounds one
thousand acres in Munster, for six hundred pounds one thousand acres in
Leinster. All according to the English measure and consisting of meadow,
arable and profitable pasture the bogs woods and barren mountains being
cast in over and above these two millions and a half of acres, to be holden
in free and common socage of the king as of his castle of Dublin.
  2. That out of these two millions and a half of acres a constant yearly rent shall be reserved to the crown of England after this proportion, viz.
out of each acre thereof in Ulster one penny, out of each acre in Connaught
three half pence, out of each acre in Munster two pence farthing, and out
of each acre in Leinster three pence, whereby his majesty's revenues out
of those lands will be much improved, besides the advantages that he will
have by the coming to his hands of all other the lands of the rebels and their
personal estates without any charge unto his majesty.
  3. That for the erecting of manors, settling of wastes and commons,
maintaining of preaching ministers, creating of corporations and regulating
of the several plantations, one or more commissions be hereafter granted
by authority of parliament.
  4. That moneys for this great occasion may be the more speedily
advanced all the undertakers in the city of London and within twenty miles
distant thereof shall underwrite their several sums before the twentieth day
of March 1641 and all within sixty miles of London before the first day of

April 1642 and the rest of the kingdom before the first day of May 1642.

5. That the several sums to be underwritten shall be paid in at four payments, viz. one fourth part within ten days after such underwriting and the other three parts at three months and three months, all to be paid into the chamber of London. . . .

And whereas as well our sovereign lord the king as the lords and commons have approved of the said propositions . . . be it therefore enacted . . . that all and every of the said propositions and every clause therein contained are and shall be according to the tenor and purport thereof hereby ratified established and confirmed with such explanations alterations and additions as in this act are expressed.

II. And be it further enacted that all and every person and persons which upon the three and twentieth day of October in the year 1641 or at any time after shall be in rebellion or levy war against the king's majesty within his realm of Ireland, or shall willingly aid, assist, or countenance any person or persons in rebellion against the king's majesty, shall lose and forfeit unto the king's majesty, his heirs and successors, all such right, title, interest, use, and possession which they or any of them, on the said three and twentieth day of October or at any time after shall have of in or unto any honours, castles, uses, possessions, offices, rights, conditions, or any other hereditaments, of what name nature or quality soever they be, and that all such right, title, interest, use, and possession, which they or any of them, or any other person or persons in trust for them, or any of them, on the said three and twentieth day of October or at any time after shall have, or of right ought to have, of, in, or to the same honours, castles, manors, messauges, rents, annuities, reversion, remainders, uses, possessions, offices, rights, conditions, or any other hereditaments, shall by the authority aforesaid, be deemed vested, adjudged, and taken to be in the actual and real possession of our sovereign lord the king, his heirs and successors, without any office or inquisition thereof. . . .

IV. And be it further enacted that John Warner, John Towse and Thomas Andrewes aldermen and Lawrence Halsted Esquire are and shall be hereby appointed and authorized to give their daily attendance at the said chamber of London to receive all such subscriptions and sums of money and to give receipts for the same. . . .

THE TREATY OF LIMERICK, 1691

Source: The Civil Articles of Limerick Exactly Printed from the Letters
          Patent (Dublin, 1692).

Articles agreed upon the third day of October 1691 between the Right
Honourable Sir Charles Porter knight and Thomas Conningsby Esq., lords
justices of Ireland, and his excellency the Baron De Ginckle, lieutenant-
general, and commander-in-chief of the English army, on the one part, and
the Right Honourable Patrick earl of Lucan, Piercy Viscount Gallmoy, Colonel
Garret Dillon, and Colonel John Brown, on the other part, in the behalf of
the Irish inhabitants in the city and county of Limerick, the counties of
Clare, Kerry, Cork, Sligo, and Mayo.

In consideration of the surrender of the city of Limerick and other
agreements made between the said Lieutenant-General Ginckle, the governor
of the city of Limerick, and the generals of the Irish army, bearing date
with these presents, for the surrender of the said city, and submission of
the said army, it is agreed, that:

1. The Roman catholics of this kingdom, shall enjoy such privileges
in the exercise of their religion, as are consistent with the laws of Ireland
or as they did enjoy in the reign of King Charles II, and their majesties'
as soon as their affairs will permit them to summon a parliament in this
kingdom, will endeavour to procure the said Roman catholics such farther
security in that particular, as may preserve them from any disturbance
upon the account of their said religion.

2. All the inhabitants or residents of Limerick, or any other garrison
now in the possession of the Irish, and all officers and soldiers, now in arms,
under any commission of King James, or those authorized by him to grant
the same in the several counties of Limerick, Clare, Kerry, Cork, and
Mayo, or any of them, and all the commissioned officers in their majesties'
quarters, that belong to the Irish regiments, now in being, that are treated
with, and who are not prisoners of war or have taken protection, and who
shall return and submit to their majesties' obedience, and their and every
of their heirs, shall hold, possess and enjoy all and every their estates of
free-hold, and inheritance, and all the rights, titles, and interests, privileges and immunities, which they, and every, or any of them held, enjoyed,
or were rightfully and lawfully entitled to in the reign of King Charles II,
or at any time since, by the laws and statutes that were in force in the said
reign of King Charles II, and shall be put in possession, by order of the
government, of such of them as are in the king's hands or the hands of his
tenants, without being put to any suit or trouble therein; and all such estates
shall be freed and discharged from all arrears of crown-rents, quit-rents,
and other public charges incurred and become due since Michaelmas 1688,
to the day of the date hereof. And all persons comprehended in this article,
shall have, hold, and enjoy all their goods and chattels, real and personal,
to them, or any of them belonging, and remaining either in their own hands,

or the hands of any persons whatsoever, in trust for or for the use of them, or any of them; and all, and every the said persons, of what profession, trade, or calling soever they be, shall and may use, exercise and practice their several and respective professions, trades and callings, as freely as they did use, exercise and enjoy the same in the reign of King Charles II, provided, that nothing in this article contained, be construed to extend to or restore any forfeiting person now out of the kingdom, except what are hereafter comprised. Provided also, that no person whatsoever shall have or enjoy the benefit of this article, that shall neglect or refuse to take the oath of allegiance made by act of parliament in England, in the first year of the reign of their present majesties, when thereunto required.

6. And whereas these present wars have drawn on great violences on both parts, and that if leave were given to the bringing all sorts of private actions, the animosities would probably continue, that have been too long on foot, and the public disturbances last; for the quieting and settling therefore of this kingdom, and avoiding those inconveniences which would be the necessary consequence of the contrary, no person or persons whatsoever, comprised in the foregoing articles, shall be sued, molested, or impleaded at the suit of any party or parties whatsoever, for any trespasses by them committed, or for any arms, horses, money, goods, chattels, merchandises, or provisions whatsoever, by them seized or taken, during the time of the war. And no person or persons whatsoever, in the second or third articles comprised, shall be sued, impleaded, or made accountable for the rents or mean rates of any lands, tenements, or houses by him or them received or enjoyed in this kingdom, since the beginning of the present war, to the day of the date hereof, nor for any waste or trespass by him or them committed in any such lands, tenements, or houses; and it is also agreed, that this article shall be mutual, and reciprocal, on both sides.

7. Every nobleman and gentleman, comprised in the said second and third article, shall have liberty to ride with a sword, and case of pistols, if they think fit, and keep a gun in their houses, for the defence of the same or for fowling.

EXCLUSION OF CATHOLICS FROM THE IRISH PARLIAMENT, 1691

Source: <u>Statutes of the Realm of England</u> (London, 1810-22), VI, 254-7.

An act for the abrogating the oath of supremacy in Ireland, and appointing other oaths

IV. And forasmuch as great disquiet and many dangerous attempts have been made, to deprive their majesties and their royal predecessors of the said realm of Ireland, by the liberty which the popish recusants there have had and taken to sit and vote in parliament, be it enacted ... that from and after the last day of January next, no person that now is, or shall be hereafter a peer of that realm, or member of the house of peers there, shall vote or make his proxy in the said house nor any person that after the said last day of January shall be a member of the house of commons, shall be capable to vote in the said house, or sit there during any debate in the same, after their speaker is chosen, until he first take the oaths herein and hereafter mentioned and expressed, and make, subscribe, and audibly repeat this declaration following:

I A.B. do solemnly and sincerely in the presence of God profess, testify, and declare, that I do believe, that in the sacrament of the Lord's supper there is not any transubstantiation of the elements of bread and wine into the body and blood of Christ, at or after the consecration thereof by any person whatsoever, and that the invocation or adoration of the Virgin Mary, or any other saint, and the sacrifice of the mass, as they are now used in the church of Rome, are superstitious and idolatrous. And I do solemnly in the presence of God, profess, testify, and declare, that I do make this declaration, and every part thereof, in the plain and ordinary sense of the words read unto me, as they are commonly understood by protestants, without any evasion, equivocation, or mental reservation whatsoever, or without any hope of any such dispensation from any person or authority whatsoever, or without believing that I am or can be acquitted before God or man, or absolved of this declaration or any part thereof, although the pope, or any person or persons, or power whatsoever, should dispense with or annul the same, or declare that it was null and void from the beginning.

V. And be it further enacted ... that if any person that now is, or hereafter shall be, a peer of Ireland, or member of the house of peers, or member of the house of commons there, or that shall become a barrister-at-law, attorney, clerk, or officer in chancery, or any other court, and all and every deputy and deputies in any office whatsoever, shall presume to offend, contrary to this act, that then every such peer and member, and such other person and persons so offending, shall be thenceforth disabled to hold or execute any office or place of profit or trust, ecclesiastical, civil or military, in any of their majesties realms of Ireland or England, or dominion of Wales, or town of Berwick-upon-Tweed, or in any of their majesty's islands or foreign plantations, to the said realms belonging; and shall be disabled from thenceforth to sit or vote in either house of parliament of the said realm of Ireland, or make a proxy in the house of peers there, or to sue or use any action, bill, plaint, or inequity, or to be guardian of any child, or executor or administrator of any person, or capable of any legacy or deed of gift, and shall forfeit, and every wilful offence against this act, the sum of five hundred pounds. . . .

A PENAL LAW, 1704

Source: Statutes at Large Passed in the Parliaments Held in Ireland, 1310-
         1800 (Dublin, 1786-1801) IV, 12-31.

An act to prevent the further growth of popery.

I. Whereas divers emissaries of the church of Rome, popish priests,
and other persons of that persuasion, taking advantage of the weakness and
ignorance of some of her majesty's subjects, or of the extreme sickness
and decay of their reason and senses, in the absence of friends and spiritual guides, do daily endeavor to persuade and pervert them from the protestant religion, to the great dishonour of Almighty God, the weakening of
the true religion, by His blessing so happily established in this realm, to
the disquieting the peace and settlement, and discomfort of many particular families thereof; and in further manifestation of their hatred and aver-
sion to the said true religion, many of the said persons so professing the
popish religion in this kingdom, have refused to make provision for their
own children for no other reason bu their being of the protestant religion;
and also by cunning devices and contrivances found out ways to avoid and
elude the intents of an act of parliament, made in the ninth year of the
reign of the late King William the Third for preventing protestants inter-
marrying with papists, and of several other laws made for the security of
the protestant religion; and whereas many persons so professing the popish
religion have it in their power to raise division among protestants, by voting in elections for members of parliament, and also have it in their power
to use other ways and means tending to the destruction of the protestant interest in this kingdom; for remedy of which great mischiefs, and to prevent the like evil practices for the future be it enacted ... that if any person or persons from and after the twenty-fourth day of March, in this present year of our Lord 1703, shall seduce, persuade or pervert any person
or persons professing, or that shall profess, the protestant religion, to
renounce, forsake, or adjure the same, and to profess the popish religion,
or reconcile him or them to the church of Rome, then and in such case
every such person or persons so seducing, as also every such protestant
or protestants who shall be so seduced, perverted and reconciled to popery,
shall for the said offences, being thereof lawfully convicted, incur the danger and penalty of praemunire, mentioned in the statute of praemunire
made in England in the sixteenth year of the reign of King Richard the Second; and if any person or persons professing the popish religion, shall
from and after the said twenty-fourth day of March send, or cause, or
willingly suffer, to be sent or conveyed any child under the age of one and
twenty years, except sailors, shipboys, or the apprentice or factor of
some merchant in trade of merchandise, into France or any other parts

beyond the seas, out of her majesty's dominions, without the special licence of her majesty, her heirs or successors or of her or their chief governor or governors of this kingdom ... he, she or they shall incur the pains, penalties and forfeitures mentioned in act made in the seventh year of his late majesty King William, entitled, <u>An act to restrain foreign education</u>.

IV. And that care may be taken for the eduction of children in the communion of the church of Ireland as by law established, be it enacted ... that no person of the popish religion shall, or may be guardian unto, or have the tuition or custody of, any orphan child or children, under the age of twenty-one years; but that the same, where the person having or entitled to the guardianship of such orphan child or children, is or shall be a papist, shall be disposed of by the high court of chancery to some near relation of such orphan child or children, being a protestant, and conforming himself to the church of Ireland as by law established, to whom the estate cannot descend, in case there shall be any such protestant relation fit to have the education of such child; otherwise to some other protestant conforming himself as aforesaid, who is hereby required to use his utmost care to educate and bring up such child or minor in the protestant religion.
...

VI. And be it further enacted ... that every papist, or person professing the popish religion, shall from and after the said twenty-fourth day of March be disabled, and is hereby made incapable, to buy and purchase either in his or in their own name, or in trust for him or her, any manor, lands, tenements, or hereditaments, or any rents or profits out of the same, or any leases or terms thereof, other than any term of years not exceeding thirty-one years, whereon a rent not less than two-thirds of the improved yearly value, at the time of the making such leases of the tenements leased, shall be reserved ....

XXIV. And for the preventing papists having it in their power to breed dissention amongst protestants by voting at elections of members of parliament; be it further enacted ... that from and after the twenty-fourth day of March 1703 no freeholder, burgess, freeman, or inhabitant of this kingdom, being a papist or professing the popish religion, shall at any time hereafter be capable of giving his or their vote for the electing of knights of any shires or counties within this kingdom, or citizens or burgesses to serve in any succeeding parliament, without first repairing to the general quarter sessions of the peace to be holden for the counties, cities, or boroughs wherein such papists do inhabit and dwell, and there voluntarilty take the oath of allegiance in the words following, viz. I A.B. do sincerely promise and swear, that I will be faithful and bear true allegiance to her majesty Queen Anne. So help me God, etc.

And also the oath of abjuration aforesaid: ....

XXVI. And whereas the superstitions of popery are greatly increased and upheld by the pretended sanctity of places, especially of a place called Saint Patrick's purgatory in the county of Donegal, and of wells, to which pilgrimages are made by vast numbers at certain seasons, by which not only the peace of the public is greatly disturbed, but the safety of the government also hazarded, by the riotous and unlawful assembling together of many thousands of papists to the said wells and other places, be it further enacted, that all such meetings and assemblies shall be deemed and adjudged riots and unlawful assemblies, and punishable as such. . . .

THE DECLARATORY ACT, 1719

Source: <u>The Statutes at Large, from Magna Charta to ... 1800</u> (London,
         1786-1800).

An act for the better securing of the dependency of the
kingdom of Ireland on the crown of Great Britain

Whereas the house of lords of Ireland have of late, against law, assumed to themselves a power and jurisdiction to examine, correct and
amend the judgments and decrees of the courts of justice in the kingdom of
Ireland; ... be it declared ... that the said kingdom of Ireland hath been,
is and of right ought to be, subordinate unto and dependent upon the imperial crown of Great Britain, as being inseparably united and annexed thereunto, and that the king's majesty, by and with the advice and consent of
the lords spiritual and temporal, and commons of Great Britain in parliament assembled, had, hath, and of right ought to have, full power and authority to make laws and statutes of sufficient force and validity to bind the
kingdom and the people of Ireland.

II. And be it further declared and enacted ... that the house of lords
of Ireland have not, nor of right ought to have, any jurisdiction to judge of,
affirm or reverse any judgment, sentence or decree, given or made in any
court within the said kingdom, and that all proceedings before the said
house of lords, upon any such judgment, sentence or decree, are, and are
hereby declared to be utterly null and void to all intents and purposes whatsoever.

EXHORTATION OF THE CATHOLIC CLERGY OF DUBLIN, 1757

Source: <u>Dublin Journal</u>, October 4, 1757.

It is now time, Christians, that you return your most grateful thanks to Almighty God, who, after visiting you with a scarcity, which approached near unto a famine, has been graciously pleased, like a merciful father, to hear your prayers, and feed you with a plentiful harvest; nor ought you to forget those kind benefactors, who in the severest times, mindful only of the public good, generously bestowed, without any distinction of persons, those large charities, by which thousands were preserved, who otherwise must have perished the victims of hunger and poverty. We ought especially to be most earnest in our thanks to the chief governors and magistrates of the kingdom, and of this city in particular, who, on this occasion, proved the fathers and saviours of the nation. But as we have not a more effectual method of shewing our acknowlegement to our temporal governors, than by an humble, peaceful, and obedient behaviour; as hitherto, we earnestly exhort you to continue in the same happy and Christian disposition, and thus, by degrees, you will entirely efface in their minds those evil impressions, which have been conceived so much to our prejudice, and industriously propagated by our enemies. A series of more than sixty years spent, with a pious resignation, under the hardships of very severe penal laws, and with the greatest thankfulness for the lenity and moderation, with which they were executed, ever since the accession of the present royal family, is certainly a fact which must outweight, in the minds of all unbiassed persons, any misconceived opinions of the doctrine and tenets of our holy church.

You know that it has always been our constant practice, as ministers of Jesus Christ, to inspire you with the greatest horror for thefts, frauds, murders, and the like abominable crimes; as being contrary to the laws of God and nature, destructive of civil society, condemned by our most holy church, which, so far from justifying them on the score of religion, or any other pretext whatsoever, delivers the unrepenting authors of such criminal practices over to Satan.

We are no less zealous than ever in exhorting you to abstain from cursing, swearing, and blaspheming; detestable vices, to which the poorer sort of our people are most unhappily addicted, and which must at one time or other bring down the vengence of heaven upon you in some visible punishment, unless you absolutely refrain from them.

It is probable, that, from hence, some people have taken occasion to brand us with this infamous calumny, that we need not fear to take false oaths, and consequently to perjure ourselves; as if we believed that any power upon earth could authorise such damnable practices, or grant dispensations for this purpose. How unjust and cruel this charge is, you know by our instructions to you both in public and private, in which we have ever condemned such doctrines, as false and impious. Others, likewise, may easily know it from the contant behaviour of numbers of Roman Catholics, who have given the strongest proofs of their abhorrence of those tenets, by refusing to take oaths, which, however conducive to their temporal interest, appeared to them entirely repugnant to the principles of their religion.

We must now intreat you, dear Christians, to offer up your most fervent prayers to the Almighty God, who holds in his hands the hearts of kings and princes, beseech him to direct the counsels of our rulers, to inspire them with sentiments of moderation and compassion towards us. We ought to be more earnest, at this juncture, in our supplications to heaven; as some very honorable personages have encouraged us to hope for a mitigation of the penal laws. Pray then the Almighty to give a blessing to these their generous designs, and to aid their counsels, in such a manner, that, whilst they intend to assist us, like kind benefactors, they may not, contrary to their intentions, by mistaking the means, most irretrievably destroy us.

To conclude, be just in your dealings, sober in your conduct, religious in your practice, avoid riots, quarrels, and tumults; and thus you will approve yourselves good citizens, peaceable subjects, and pious Christians.

WHITEBOY OATH, 1762

Source: W. W. Seward, <u>Collectanea Hibernica</u>, Dublin; Stewart and Butler, 1812, I, 30-1.

I do hereby solemnly and sincerely swear, that I will not make known any secret now given me, or that hereafter may be given me, to any one in the world, except a sworn person belonging to the society called <u>White-boys</u>, or otherwise, <u>Sive Ultagh's</u> children.

Furthermore I swear, that I will be ready at an hour's warning (if possible) being properly summoned by any of the officers, serjeants, or corporals belonging to my company.

Furthermore I swear, that I will not wrong any of the company I belong to, of the value of one shilling; nor suffer it to be done by others, without acquainting them thereof.

Furthermore I swear, I will not make known in any shape whatsoever, to any person that does not belong to us, the name or names of any of our fraternity; but particularly the name of our respective officers.

Lastly I swear, that I will not drink of any liquor whatsoever, whilst on duty, without the consent of one or other of the officers, serjeants or corporals; and that we will be loyal one to the other, as far as in our power lies.

THE VICEROY'S FAREWELL TO PARLIAMENT, 1772

Source: "Speech of His Excellency George Lord Viscount Townshend, Lord Lieutenant-General, and General-Governor of Ireland, to both Houses of Parliament . . . the 2d day of June, 1772," Annual Register, London: J. Dodsley, 1773, pp. 231-2.

My Lords, and Gentlemen,

It gives me great pleasure to observe that the tumults and outrages of the lower ranks of people, which unhappily disturbed some of the northern counties of this kingdom, have now subsided. I flatter myself that these deluded persons are fully convinced of the atrociousness of their attempts, and of the impossibility of effecting any of the purposes intended by them. I would however recommend it to such gentlemen whose weight and influence lie particularly in those parts to have a watchful eye over their behaviour, and to exert themselves, with the other civil magistrates, in enforcing a due obedience to the laws; and I doubt not that, by their authority on one hand, and by their justice and moderation on the other, a thorough reformation will be effected; and the dispositions of the people reclaimed to peace and good order.

It gives me great concern to see the assistance of the military power so frequently called for; nothing can be more worthy of your serious reflection than to render that resource unnecessary by a judicious improvement of your police, and providing for a due execution of the laws.

His majesty gave it in express command to me to make your interests and prosperity the great objects of my administration; and my own inclinations incited me to a strict and zealous performance of that duty. I have, upon every occasion, endeavoured, to the utmost of my power, to promote the public service; and I feel the most perfect satisfaction in now repeating to you my acknowledgements for the very honourable manner in which (after a residence of near five years amongst you) you have declared your entire approbation of my conduct. Be assured that I shall always entertain the most ardent wishe for your welfare; and shall make a faithful representation to his majesty of your loyalty and attachment to his royal person and government.

THE GROWTH OF SECTARIAN VIOLENCE, 1784-95

Source: W. W. Seward, Collectanea Hibernica, Dublin: Stewart and Butler, 1812, III, 153-4.

As a great conflagration is often kindled by a small spark, so the feuds and altercations between the peep-of-day boys and defenders, the former Presbyterians, the latter Romanists, which occasioned much strife and bloodshed, have been ascribed to a triffling dispute between two individuals.

On the fourth of July, 1784, two men of the former persuasion had a quarrel and fought near Market-hill, a small town in the county of Armagh, when one of the combatants became victorious, by the advice and assistance of a Roman Catholic peasant, and his brother, who happened to be present, for which the vanquished hero vowed vengeance against the latter.

A second challenge took place, but the two Romanists would not attend the combat, having been informed, that the Presbyterians, who had been defeated, resolved to be revenged of him and his party.

At last the vanquished Presbyterian published, that a horse-race would take place on a certain day at Hamilton's-bawn, where the combatants met and fought a second time; when the conqueror became victorious by the assistance of some Romanists who fought on his side. Both parties began to raise recruits, and to collect arms; but Presbyterians and Papists mixed indiscriminately, and were marked for some by the district to which they belonged, and not by any religious distinction. Each body assumed the singular appelation of fleet, and was denominated from the parish or town-land where the persons who composed it resided.

The Nappack fleet was at first headed by a Roman Catholic; and the people in the neighborhood of Bunker's-hill (in the road from Newry to Armagh,) entered into an association to defend themselves against the Nappack fleet, chose a dissenting minister for their leader, assumed, for the first time, the title of defenders, and were joined soon after by the Bawn fleet, in order to protect themselves against the Nappack fleet. On Whit-sunday, in the year 1795, the two parties met, and were to have had a desperate engagement.

The Nappack fleet, 700 in number, were all armed with guns, sword, and pistols. The Bunker's-hill defenders, and the Bawn fleet, though much more numerous, were not so well armed. When they were on the point of engaging, Mr. Richardson, of Richhill, member for the county of Armagh, and two more gentlemen, interposed, and induced them to separate, which prevented a great effusion of blood.

From the inveterate hatred which has ever existed between the two sects, they soon began to separate, and to enlist under the banners of religion; and as the Roman Catholics shewed uncommon eagerness to collect arms, the Presbyterians began to disarm them.

JOHN FITZGIBBON ON THE REGENCY QUESTION, IRISH HOUSE OF
COMMONS, FEBRUARY 11, 1789

Source: <u>Parliamentary Register</u> (Dublin, 1790), IX. 48-9.

I shall in as few words as possible state my opinion. And first I
maintain that the crown of Ireland and the corwn of England are inseparably
and indissolubly united. Secondly, I do maintain, that the Irish parliament
is perfectly and totally independent of the British parliament.

The first position is your security; the second is your freedom; and
when gentlemen talk any other language than this, they either talk to the
separation of the crowns, or the subjugation of your parliament; they invade either your security or your liberty; further, the only security of
your liberty is your connexion with Great Britain, and gentlemen who risk
breaking the connexion must make up their mind to a union. God forbid I
should ever see that day; but if ever the day on which a separation shall be
attempted, may come, I shall not hesitate to embrace a union rather than
a separation.

Under the Duke of Portland's government the grievances of Ireland
were stated to be, the alarming usurpation of the British parliament, a perpetual mutiny bill, and the powers assumed by the privy council.

These grievances were redressed, and in redressing them you passed a law repealing part of Pynings'. By your new law you enact, that all
bills which pass the two houses here, which shall be certified into England,
and shall be returned under the great seal of England, without any addition,
diminuition, or alteration whatsoever, shall pass into law, and no other.
By this you make the great seal of England essentially and indispensably
necessary on the passing of laws in Ireland, you can pass no act without
first certifying it into England, and having it returned under the great seal
of that kingdom, insomuch that were the king of England and Ireland to
come here in person and reside, he could not pass a bill without it first
being certified to his regent in England, who must return it under the seal
of that kingdom before his majesty could even in person assent to it. This
bill was framed and introduced by a gentleman, certainly of as good intentions as any man in the kingdom. By this bill the great seal of England is
the organ by which the king of England speaks, and it is nonsense to say,
that it is as king of Ireland he affixes the great seal of England to Irish
acts, as well might you say that it is as king of Ireland he affixes the great
seal of England to treaties of peace, alliance or commerce, which nevertheless include Ireland. I have stated, that his majesty could not, were he
here in person, pass an act without having first the great seal of England
affixed thereto. Let me now for a moment suppose, that we, in the dignity
of our independence, appoint a regent for Ireland, being a different person
from the regent of England, a case not utterly impossible, if the gentlemen

insist on appointing the prince of Wales before it will be known whether he shall accept the regency of England; and suppose we should go further, and desire him to give the royal assent to bills, he would say 'My good people of Ireland, you here by your own law made the great seal of England absolutely and essentially necessary to be affixed to each bill before it passes in Ireland, that seal is in the hands of the chancellor of England, who is a very sturdy fellow, that chancellor is an officer under the regent of England, I have no manner of authority over him, and so, my very good people, of Ireland, you had better apply to the regent of England, and request that he will order the chancellor of England to affix the great seal of England to your bills, otherwise, my very good people of Ireland, I cannot pass them; ....

AN ACT MORE EFFECTUALLY TO SUPPRESS INSURRECTIONS, AND PREVENT THE DISTURBANCE OF THE PUBLIC PEACE
1796

Source: Statutes at Large Passed in the Parliaments Held in Ireland, 1310 1800 (Dublin, 1786-1801), XVII, 978-90.

Whereas traitorous insurrections have for some time past arisen in various parts of this kingdom, principally promoted and supported by persons associating under the pretended obligation of oaths unlawfully administered ... be it enacted ... that any person or persons who shall administer, or cause to be administered, or be present, aiding and assisting at the administering, or who shall by threats, promises, persuasions, or other undue means, cause, procure, or induce to be taken by any person or persons, upon a book, or otherwise any oath or engagement, importing to bind the person taking the same, to be of any association, brotherhood, society, or confederacy formed for seditious purposes, or to disturb the public peace, or to obey the orders or rules, or commands of any captain, leader, or commander (not appointed by his majesty, his heirs or successors) or to assemble at the desire or command of any such captain, leader, commander or committee, or of any person or persons not having lawful authority, or not to inform or give evidence against any brother, associate, confederate, or other person, or not to reveal or discover his having taken any illegal oath, or done any illegal act, or not to discover any illegal oath or engagement which may be tendered to him, or the import thereof, whether he shall take such oath, or enter into such engagement, or not, being by due course of law conviceted thereof, shall be adjudged guilty of felony, and suffer death without benefit of clergy, and every person who shall take any such oath or engagement, not being thereto compelled by inevitable necessity, and being by due course of law thereof convicted, shall be adjudged guilty of felony and be transported for life.

VI. And be it further enacted, that all persons who shall have arms in their possession at any time after the passing of this act, shall on or before the first day of May 1796, or immediately after they shall have possession of such arms, deliver to the acting clerk of the peace in the county, town, or city in which he resides ... a written notification, signed by him or her, specifying therein ... the place or places where the same are usually kept, accompanied by an affidavit, sworn by the person signing such notification, that the notification is true, and that he believes he is by law entitled to keep arms ....

VIII. And be it enacted, that any person having arms, and not making such registry as aforesaid, shall upon being convicted thereof, on the testimony of two credible witnesses on oath before any magistrate, for the first offense forfeit the sum of ten pounds ... or be imprisoned by such magistrate for the space of two months, and for the second and every other offence shall in like manner forfeit the sum of twenty pounds, or be imprisoned for the space of four months.

X.   And be it further enacted, that it shall and may be lawful for any justice of the peace, or for any person authorized thereto by warrant under the hand of any justice of the peace, to search for arms in the houses or grounds of any person not having made such notification as aforesaid, and whom he shall have reasonable ground to suspect of having arms, and also in the houses or grounds of any person who having made such notification, shall refuse or neglect to deliver such list or inventory, or whom he shall have reasonable ground to suspect to have delivered a false list or inventory, and in case of refusal of admission, to break into such house and every part thereof by force, and if any arms shall be found in the possession of any such person respectively, to seize and carry away the same for the use of his majesty.

XII.   And whereas in several instances persons who have given information against persons accused of crime have been murdered before trial of the persons accused, in order to prevent their giving evidence and to effect the acquittal of the accused, and some magistrates have been assassinated for their exertions in bringing offenders to justice, be it declared and enacted, that if any person who hath given or shall give information or examinations upon oath against any person or persons for any offence against the laws, shall after the twentieth day of February 1796 and before the trial of the person or persons against whom such information or examination hath been or shall be given, be murdered or violently put to death, or so maimed or forcibly carried away and secreted as not to be able to give evidence on the trial of the person or persons against whom such information or examinations were given, the information or examination or such person to take on oath, shall be admitted as evidence on the trial of the person or persons against whom such information or examination was given.

XV.   And be it further enacted, that it shall and may be lawful for any justice of the peace to arrest and bring before him, or cause to be arrested or brought before him, any stranger sojourning or wandering, and to examine him on oath respecting his place of abode, the place from whence he came, his manner of livelihood, and his object or motive for remaining or coming into the county, town or city, in which he shall be found, and unless he shall answer to the satisfaction of such magistrate, such magistrate shall commit him to gaol or the house of correction, there to remain until he find surety for his good behaviour.

XVI.   And in order to restore peace to such parts of the kingdom as are or may be disturbed by seditious persons, be it further enacted, that it shall and may be lawful to and for any two justices of the peace ... to summon a special session of the peace ... to consider the state of the county ... and that the justices assembled in consequence, not being fewer than seven, or the major part of them, one of whom to be of the quorum, or if in a county or a town or city, not being fewer than three, shall and may if they see fit ... signify by memorial signed by them to the lord lieutenant or other chief governor or governors of this kingdom, that they consider their county or any part thereof,to be in a state of disturbance or in immediate danger of becoming so, and thereupon it shall and may be lawful to and for the lord lieutenant or other chief governor or governors of this kingdom, by and with the advice of his majesty's privy council by proclamation to declare such county, or any part of such county, to be in a state of disturbance or in immediate danger of becoming so, and also such parts of any adjoining county or counties as such chief governor or governors and council shall think fit, in order to prevent the continuance or extension of such disturbance.

XVII.   And be it further enacted, that within three days after such proclamation made, or as soon after as may be, every clerk of the peace of every part of the district proclaimed, shall respectively in his county, give notice of holding within two days, or as soon after as may be, a petty session of the peace, and the justices of the peace shall pursuant to such notice assemble ... and the said justices at said first meeting shall order and direct a notification signed by them to be made throughout the district so proclaimed, that such district has been so proclaimed, and commanding the inhabitants to keep within their dwellings at all unseasonable times between sun-set and sun-rise, and warning them of the penalties to which a contrary conduct will expose them ...

XVIII.   And be it further enacted, that it shall and may be lawful to and for any magistrate or other peace officer within such district, after such notification shall be made as aforesaid, to arrest or cause to be arrested any person who shall within such district be found in the fields, streets, highways, or elsewhere out of his dwelling or place of abode, at any time from one hour after sun-set until sun-rise and to bring him before two justices of the peace ... and unless he can prove to their satisfaction that he was out of his house upon his lawful occasions, such person shall be deemed an idle and disorderly person, and shall be transmitted by the warrant of such justices to the officer at some port appointed to receive recruits for his majesty's navy, by which officer such person shall be received as a recruit for his majesty's navy, and transmitted to serve on board his majesty's navy.

XIX.   Provided always, that it shall and may be lawful to and for every such person so arrested, to appeal to the next sessions of the peace ...

XXII.   And be it enacted ... that persons who cannot upon examination prove themselves to exercise and industriously follow some lawful trade or employment as a labourer or otherwise, or to have some substance sufficient for their support or maintenance, shall be deemed idle and disorderly persons, and shall be dealt with according to what is herein before directed respecting persons out of their dwellings at unreasonable hours aforesaid.

XXIX. And be it further enacted, that it shall and may be lawful for any justice of the peace, or any person authorized by the warrant of such justice in any district so proclaimed and whilst such proclaimation shall remain in force, to call upon every person who has registered arms within such district to produce or account for the same, and to enter any house or place whatever, and search for arms and ammunition, and to take and carry away all arms and ammunition which they may think necessary to take possession of, in order to preserve or restore the public peace ....

XXXI. And be it further enacted, that all persons found assembled in any proclaimed district, in any house in which malt or spirituous liquors are sold, not being inmates thereof or travellers, whether licensed or unlicensed, after the hours of nine at night and before six in the morning, shall be liable to be deemed idle and disorderly persons within the meaning of this act ...

XXXII. And be it further enacted, that if any man or boy shall, in any district so proclaimed, hawk or disperse any seditious handbill, paper or pamphlet, or paper by law required to be stamped and not duly stamped, such man or boy shall be deemed an idle and disorderly person, and dealt with accordingly, and as in herein before directed; and if any woman shall hawk or disperse any seditious hand-bill, paper, or paper not duly stamped, such woman being convicted thereof by the oath of one witness before two justices of the peace, one of whom to be of the quorum, such woman shall by the warrant of such two justices be committed to the gaol of the county, there to remain for three months, unless she shall sooner discover the person or persons from whom she received or by whom she was employed to sell, hawk or disperse such papers or pamphlets, provided always, that such woman may appeal from such adjudication to the next sessions of the peace.

XXXVII. Provided always ... that when a verdict shall be given for the plaintiff in any action to be brought against any justice of the peace, peace officer or other person, for taking or imprisoning or detaining any person, or for seizing arms or ammunition, or entering houses under colour of any authority given by this act, and it shall appear to the judge or judges before whom the same shall be tried, that there was a probable cause for doing the act complained of in such action, and the judge or court shall certify the same on record, then in that case the plaintiff shall not be entitled to more than sixpence damages, nor to any costs of suit.

XXXVII. Provided also, that where a verdict shall be given for the plaintiff in any such action as aforesaid, and the judge or court before whom the cause shall be tried, shall certify on the record that the injury for which such action is brought was wilfully and maliciously committed, the plaintiff shall be entitled to double costs of suit.

THE UNITED IRISHMEN, 1797

Source: <u>Journals of the House of Commons of the Kingdom of Ireland,
1613-1800</u> (Dublin, 1796-1800), XVII, Appendix, pp. 888-9.

The declaration, resolutions, and constitution of the
societies of United Irishmen

In the present era of reform, when unjust governments are falling in
every quarter of Europe, when religious persecution is compelled to abjure
her tyranny over conscience, when the rights of men are ascertained in
theory, and that theory substantiated by practice, when antiquity can no
longer defend absurd and oppressive forms, against the common sense and
common interests of mankind, when all governments are acknoweldged to
originate from the people, and to be so far only obligatory, as they protect their rights, and promote their welfare, we think it our duty, as Irishmen, to come forward, and state what we feel to be our heavy grievance,
and what we know to be its effectural remedy. We have no national government, we are ruled by Englishmen, and the servants of Englishmen, whose
object is the interest of another country, whose instrument is corruption,
and whose strength is the weakness of Ireland; and these men have the
whole of the power and patronage of the country, as means to seduce and
subdue the honesty of her representatives in the legislature. Such an ex-
trinsic power, acting with uniform force, in a direction too frequently op-
posite to the true line of our obvious interest, can be resisted with effect
solely by unanimity, decision, and spirit in the people, qualities which
may be exerted most legally, constitutionally, and efficaciously, by that
great measure, essential to the prosperity and freedom of Ireland, an
equal representation of all the people in parliament.

Impressed with these sentiments, we have agreed to form an association, to be called the Society of United Irishmen, and we do pledge ourselves to our country, and mutually to each other, that we will steadily
support, and endeavour by all due means to carry into effect the following
resolutions;

1st. Resolved, That the weight of English influence in the government
of this country is so great, as to require a cordial union among all the
people of Ireland, to maintain that balance which is essential to the preservation of our liberties, and extenstion of our commerce.

2nd. That the sole constitutional mode by which this influence can
be opposed is by a complete and radical reform of the representation of
the people in parliament.

3rd. That no reform is practicable, efficacious, or just, which
shall not include Irishmen of every religious persuasion.

Satisfied, as we are, that the intestine divisions among Irishmen have too often given encouragement and impunity to profligate, audacious, and corrupt administrations, in measures which, but for these divisions, they durst not have attempted, we submit our resolutions to the nation, as the basis of our political faith. We have gone to what we conceived to be the evil. We have stated what we conceive to be remedy. With a parliament thus formed, everything is easy -- without it, nothing can be done -- and we do call on, and most earnestly exhort our countrymen in general to follow our example, and to form similar societies in every quarter of the kingdom, for the promotion of constitutional knowledge, the abolition of bigotry in religion and politics, and the equal distribution of Irishmen. The people, when thus collected, will feel their own weight, and secure that power which theory has already admitted as their portion, and to which, if they be not aroused by their present provocations to vindicate it, they deserve to forfeit their pretensions for ever.

1st. This society is constituted for the purpose of forwarding a brotherhood of affection, a community of rights, and a union of power among Irishmen of every religious persuasion; and thereby to obtain a complete reform in the legislature, founded on the principles of civil, political, and religious liberty.

2nd. Every candidate for admission into this society shall be proposed by one member and seconded by another, both of whom shall vouch for his character and principles. The candidate to be ballotted for on the society's subsequent meeting, and if one of the beans shall be black, he shall stand rejected.

3rd. Each society shall fix upon a weekly subscription suited to the circumstances and convenience of its numbers, which they shall regularly return to their baronial by the proper officer.

4th. The officers of this society shall be a secretary and treasurer, who shall be appointed by ballot every three months: on every first meeting in November, February, May and August.

5th. A society shall consist of no more than twelve members, and those as nearly as possible of the same street or neighbourhood, whereby they may be all thoroughly known to each other, and their conduct be subject to the censorial check of all.

6th. Every person elected a member of this society shall, previous to his admission, take the following test. But in order to diminish risk, it shall be taken in a separate apartment, in the presence of the persons who proposed and seconded him, only, after which the new member shall be brought into the body of the society, and there vouched for by the same.

TEST

In the awful presence of God, I, A.B., do voluntarily declare, that I will persevere in endeavouring to form a brotherhood of affection among Irishmen of every religious persuasion, and that I will also persevere in my endeavours to obtain an equal, full, and adequate representation of all the people of Ireland. I do further declare, that neither hopes, fears, rewards, or punishments, shall ever induce me, directly or indirectly, to inform on, or give evidence against, any member or members of this or similar societies for any act or expression of theirs, done or made collectively or individually in or out of this society, in pursuance of the spirit of this obligation.

RULES OF THE ORANGE SOCIETY, 1798

Source: <u>Report</u> <u>from</u> <u>the</u> <u>Select</u> <u>Committe</u> (of the House of Commons) . . .
to <u>Inquire</u> <u>into</u> <u>the</u> <u>Nature</u> . . . of <u>Orange</u> <u>Lodges</u> . . . in <u>Ireland</u>. . . . London: Hansard, 1835, XV, 2.

1. General declaration of the objects of the Orange Institution

We associate to the utmost of our power to support and defend His
Majesty, George III, the constitution, and laws of this country, and the
succession to the throne in His Majesty's illustrious House, being Protestant; for the defence of our persons and properties, and to maintain
the peace of our country; and for these purposes, we will be at all times
ready to assist the civil and military powers, in the just and lawful dis-
charge of their duty. We also associate in honour of King William III,
Prince of Orange, whose name we bear, as supporters of his glorious
memory, and the true religion by him completely established; and in order
to prove our gratitude and affection for his name, we will annually cele-
brate the victory over James at the Boyne on the 1st day of July (O.S.) in
every year, which day shall be our grand day for ever.

We further declare, that we are exclusively a Protestant association,
yet detesting as we do any intolerant spirit, we solemnly pledge ourselves
to each other, that we will not persecute or upbraid any person on account
of his religious opinion, but that we will, on the contrary, be aiding and
assisting to every loyal subject of every religious description.

2. Qualifications requisite for an Orangeman

He should have a sincere love and veneration for his Almighty Maker,
productive of those lively and happy fruits, righteousness and obedience to
his commands; a firm and steady faith in the Saviour of the world, convinced that He is the only mediator between a sinful creature and an
offended Creator; Without those he can be no Christian -- of an humane
and compassionate disposition, and a courteous and affable behaviour.
He should be an enemy to savage brutality and unchristian cruelty; a lover
of society and improving company; and have a laudable regard for the
Protestant religion, and a sincere regard to propagate its precepts; zealous
in promoting the honour of his King and country; heartily desirous of
victory and success in those pursuits, yet convinced and assured that God
alone can grant them; he should have an hatred of cursing and swearing,
and taking the name of God in vain (a shameful practice); he should use all
opportunities of discouraging it among his brethren; wisdom and prudence
should guide his actions, honesty and integrity direct his conduct, and
honour and glory be the motives of his endeavours. Lastly, he should
pay the strictest attention to a religious observance of the Sabbath, and
also of temperance and sobriety.

3. Obligation of an Orangeman

I . . . do solemnly and sincerely swear of my own free will and accord, that I will, to the utmost of my power, support and defend the present King, George III, and all the heirs of the Crown, so long as he or they support the Protestant ascendancy, the constitution, and laws of these kingdoms; and I do further swear that I am not, nor was ever a Roman Catholic or papist; that I was not, am not, nor ever will be, an United Irishman, and that I never took an oath of secrecy to that society; and I do further swear in the presence of Almighty God that I will always conceal, and never reveal, either part or parts of this that I am about now to receive, neither write it, nor stamp, stain, nor engrave it, now cause it to be done, on paper, parchment, leaf, bark, brick, stone, or anything so that it might be known; and that I am now become an Orangeman, without fear, bribery, or corruption.

4. Marksman obligation

I . . . of my own free will and accord, in the presence of Almighty God, do hereby most solemnly and sincerely swear, that I will always conceal, and never reveal, either part or parts of this which I am about to receive, and that I will bear true allegiance to His Majesty, George III, and all the heirs of the Crown, as long as they maintain the Protestant ascendancy, the laws and constitution of these kingdoms; and that I will keep this part of a Marksman from that of an Orangeman, as well as from the ignorant, and so will not make a man until I become Master of a body nor after I am broke; and that I will not make a man or be present at the making of a man, on the road, or behind hedges, and that I will be aiding and assisting to all true Orange honest Marksmen, as far as it is in my power, knowing him or them to be such, and that I will not wrong a brother Marksman, nor know him to be wronged of anything of value worth apprehending, but I will warn and apprize him of it if in my power it lies. All this I swear with a firm and stedfast resolution, so help me God, and keep me stedfast in this, my Marksman obligation.

5. Secret articles of the lodges

i. That we will bear true allegiance to His Majesty, George III, and his successors so long as he or they support the Protestant ascendancy, and we will faithfully support and maintain the laws and constitution of this kingdom.

ii. That we will be true to all Orangemen in all just actions, neither wronging nor seeing him wronged to our knowledge without acquainting him thereof.

iii. That we are not to see a brother offended for six pence or one shilling, or more, if convenient, which must be returned next meeting, if possible.

iv. We must not give the first assault to any person whatever, that may bring a brother into trouble.

v. We are not to carry away money, goods, or anything from any person whatever, except arms and ammunition, and those only from the enemy.

vi. We are to appear in ten hours' warning, or whatever time is required; if possible, but provided it is not hurtful to ourselves and family, and that we are served with a lawful summons from the master, otherwise we are fined as the company may think fit.

vii. No man may be made an Orangeman without the unanimous approbation of the body.

viii. An Orangeman is to keep a brother's secret as his own, unless in case of murder, treason or perjury, and that of his own free will.

ix. No Roman Catholic can be admitted on any account.

x. Any Orangeman who acts contrary to these rules shall be expelled, and the same reported to all Lodges in this Kingdom and elsewhere.

THE ACT OF UNION, 1800

Source: <u>Statutes at Large Passed in the Parliaments Held in Ireland, 1310-1800</u> (Dublin, 1786-1801), XX, 448-87.

An act for the union of Great Britain and Ireland

I. That it be the first article of the union of the kingdoms of Great Britain and Ireland, that the said kingdom of Great Britain and Ireland shall, upon the first day of January, which shall be in the year of our Lord 1801, and for ever, be united into one kingdom, by the name of 'The United Kingdom of Great Britain and Ireland, ' and that the royal style and titles appertaining to the imperial crown of the said united kingdom and its dependencies, and also the ensigns, armorial flags, and banners thereof, shall be such as his majesty by his royal proclamation under the great seal of the united kingdom shall be pleased to appoint.

II. That it be the second article of union, that the succession to the imperial crown of the said united kingdom, and of the dominions thereunto belonging, shall continue limited and settled in the same manner as the succession to the imperial crown of the said kingdoms of Great Britain and Ireland now stands limited and settled, according to the existing laws, and to the terms of union between England and Scotland.

III. That it be the third article of union, that the said united kingdom be represented in one and the same parliament, to be styled 'The parliament of the United Kingdom of Great Britain and Ireland. '

IV. That it be the fourth article of union that four lords spiritual of Ireland, by rotation of sessions, and twenty-eight lords temporal of Ireland, elected for life by the peers of Ireland, shall be the number to sit and vote on the part of Ireland in the house of lords of the parliament of the united kingdom, and one hundred commoners (two for each county of Ireland, two for the city of Dublin, two for the city of Cork, one for the University of Trinity college, and one for each of the thirty-one most considerable cities, towns, and boroughs) be the number to sit and vote on the part of Ireland in the house of commons of the parliament of the united kingdom. . . .

ROBERT EMMET'S REBELLION, 1803

Source: Annual Register, London: J. Stockdale, 1804, pp. 90-92.

By the Lord-Lieutenant and Council of Ireland.
A Proclamation.

HARDWICKE.

Whereas divers person, engaged in a treasonable and daring insurrection against his majesty's government, did, on the evening of yesterday, the 23rd of July inst. suddenly assemble in the liberties of Dublin,
with fire-arms and pikes and did there commit several outrages, and
particularly in Thomas street, in the parish of St. Catharine, within the
said liberties, did assault the carriage of the right honourable Arthur
lord viscount Kilwarden, chief justice of his majesty's court of king's
bench, and one of his majesty's most honourable privy council, and did
drag the said Arthur lord Viscount Kilwarden, together with his nephew
the rev. Richard Wolfe, clerk, from his said carriage, and did there basely
and inhumanly murder the said Arthur lord viscount Kilwarden and Richard
Wolfe, by stabbing them respectively with pikes in various parts of their
bodies, of which wounds they both soon after died.

Now we, the lord-lieutenant and council, in order to bring such
enormous offenders to condign punishment, do, by this our proclamation,
publish and declare, that if any person or persons shall, within six calen-
dar months from the date hereof, discover any of the person or persons
who committed the said inhuman murders on the said Arthur viscount
Kilwarden, and the said rev. Richard Wolfe, or either of them, or who
aided and assisted therein, or who advised, encouraged, instigated, moved,
stimulated, or incited the persons concerned therein to commit the same,
such person or persons so discovering shall receive as a reward the sum
of one thousand pounds sterling for each and every of the first three persons who shall be apprehended and convicted thereof.

And we do likewise publish and declare, that if any of the persons
concerned in the murders aforesaid, save and except the persons who
actually stabbed the said lord viscount Kilwarden and the rev. Richard
Wolfe, or either of them, as aforesaid, shall discover any other of the
persons concerned in the said murders, or either of them, so that such
person or persons so discovering shall be convicted thereof, such person
or persons so discovering, shall, over and above the said reward, receive
his majesty's most gracious pardon for said offences.

And whereas it has appeared to us, that the daring and rebellious
outrages aforesaid were committed in prosecution of a rebellious conspiracy against his majesty's government, and that divers other enormities
were at the same time committed in Thomas-street aforesaid, and in
the neighbourhood thereof, in prosecution of the same treasonable purpose, and that divers of the persons engaged therein, did come to Dublin
with intent to commit such outrages and enormities, in order to induce and

persuade his majesty's peaceable and loyal subjects in the city of Dublin and its neighbourhood, by the tenor thereof, and by apprehensions for their own personal safety, to join in the treasonable conspiracy aforesaid.

Now we, the lord-lieutenant and council, do hereby strictly enjoin and command all his majesty's subjects, in their several stations and according to their several duties, to use their utmost endeavours to suppress all such rebellious insurrections and treasonable practices, and to apprehend and bring the persons engaged therein to the punishment due to their crimes; and more especially we do strictly enjoin and command the lord mayor of the city of Dublin, and all the justices of the peace of the said city of Dublin, and of the county of Dublin, and all sheriffs and other magistrates and officers within their several jurisdictions, and all other his majesty's loving subjects, to do all acts in their power to such purposes.

And we do hereby further require and command all officers commanding his majesty's forces to employ the troops under their command in the most speedy and effectual manner for the suppression of all rebellious insurrections and treasonable practices, wherever the same may appear; and particularly to disarm all rebels, and recover all arms forcibly and traitorously taken from his majesty's peaceable and loyal subjects, and take up and seize all arms and ammunition which may be found in the custody of any person or persons not duly authorised by law to have and keep the same.

Given at the council chamber, in Dublin, the 24th day of July, 1803. Signed, Redesdale C., Chas. Dublin, W. Tuam, Drogheda, Ely, Arran, Annesley, Tyrawley, Her. Langrishe, Denis Browne, Henry King, S. Hamilton, St. George Daly, D. La Touche, James Fitzgerald, M. Fitzgerald, H. E. Fox, M. Smith, Standish O'Grady.

GOD SAVE THE KING

CATHOLIC EMANCIPATION, 1829

Source: <u>Public General Statutes</u> (London, 1832-67, 1829, pp. 105-15.)

An act for the relief of his majesty's Roman Catholic subjects

Whereas by various acts of parliament certain restraints and disabilities are imposed on the Roman catholic subjects of his majesty, to which other subjects of his majesty are not liable, and whereas it is expedient that such restraints and disabilities shall be from henceforth discontinued, and whereas by various acts certain oaths and certain declarations, commonly called the declarations against transubstantiation and the invocation of saints and the sacrifice of the mass, as practised in the church of Rome, are or may be required to be taken, made, and subscribed, by the subjects of his majesty, as qualification for sitting and voting in parliament, and for the enjoyment of certain offices, franchises, and civil rights, be it enacted ... that from and after the commencement of this act all such parts of the said acts as require the said declarations, or either of them, to be made or subscribed by any of his majesty's subjects, as a qualification for sitting and voting in parliament, or for the exercise or enjoyment of any office, franchise, or civil right, be and the same are (save as hereinafter provided and excepted) hereby repealed.

II. And be it enacted, that ... it shall be lawful for any person professing the Roman catholic religion, being a peer, or who shall after the commencement of this act be returned as a member of the house of commons, to sit and vote in either house of parliament respectively, being in all other respects duly qualified to sit and vote therein, upon taking and subscribing the following oath, instead of the oaths of allegiance, supremacy, and abjuration: I, A.B., do sincerely promise and swear, that I will be faithful and bear true allegiance to his majesty King George the fourth, and will defend him to the utmost of my power against all conspiracies and attempts whatever, which shall be made against his person, crown, or dignity. And I will do my utmost endeavour to disclose and make known to his majesty, his heirs and successors, all treasons and traitorous conspiracies which may be formed against him or them. And I do faithfully promise to maintain, support, and defend, to the utmost of my power, the succession of the crown, which succession, by an act, entitled <u>An act for the further limitation of the crown, and better securing the rights and liberties of the subject,</u> is and stands limited to the Princess Sophia, electress of Hanover, and the heirs of her body, being protestants; hereby utterly renouncing and abjuring any obedience or allegiance unto any other person claiming or pretending a right to the crown of this realm. And I do further declare, that it is not an article of my faith, and that I do renounce, reject, and abjure the opinion, that princes excommunicated or deprived by the pope, or any

other authority of the see of Rome, may be deposed or murdered by their
subjects, or by any person whatsoever. And I do declare, that I do not believe that the pope of Rome, or any other foreign prince, prelate, person,
state, or potentate, hath or ought to have any temporal or civil jurisdiction,
power, superiority, or pre-eminence, directly or indirectly, within this
realm. I do swear, that I will defend to the utmost of my power the settlement of property within this realm, as established by the laws, and I do
hereby disclaim, disavow, and solemnly abjure, any intention to subvert
the present church establishment as settled by law within this realm, and
I do solemnly swear, that I never will exercise any privilege to which I am
or may become entitled, to disturb or weaken the protestant religion or
protestant government in the United Kingdom. And I do solemnly, in the
presence of God profess, testify, and declare, that I do make this declaration and every part thereof, in the plain and ordinary sense of the words of
this oath, without any evasion, equivocation, or mental reservation whatsoever. So help me God.

V. And be it further enacted, that it shall be lawful for persons professing the Roman catholic religion to vote at elections of members to
serve in parliament for England and for Ireland, and also to vote at the
elections of representative peers of Scotland and of Ireland, and to be elected such representative peers, being in all other respects duly qualified,
upon taking and subscribing the oath hereinbefore appointed and set forth
. . .

X. And be it enacted, that it shall be lawful for any of his majesty's
subjects professing the Roman catholic religion to hold, exercise and enjoy, all civil and military offices and places of trust or profit under his
majesty, his heirs or successors; and to exercise any other franchise or
civil right, except as hereinafter excepted, upon taking and subscribing ..
the oath hereinbefore appointed. . . . .

O'CONNELL AND THE REPEAL CAMPAIGN:
SPEECH AT MULLINGAR, 1843

Source: The Nation, May 20, 1843.

My first object is to get Ireland for the Irish (loud cheers). I am
content that the English should have England, but they have had the domination of this country too long, and it is time that the Irish should at length
get their own country -- that they should get the management of their own
country -- the regulation of their own country -- the enjoyment of their own
country -- that the Irish should have Ireland (great cheers). Nobody can
known how to govern us as well as we would know how to do it ourselves --
nobody could know how to relieve our wants as well as we would ourselves
-- nobody could have so deep an interest in our prosperity, happiness for
us as we would ourselves (hear, hear). Old Ireland and liberty! (loud
cheers). That is what I am struggling for (hear, hear). If I was to tell the
Scotch that they should not have Scotland -- if I was to tell the English that
they should not have England -- if I was to tell the Spaniards that they
should not have Spain -- or the French that they should not have France,
they would have a right to laugh at, to hate, to attack, or to assail me in
whatever manner they chose. But I do not say any such thing. What I say
is, that as all these people have their own countries, the Irish ought to have
Ireland (hear, and cheers). What numberless advantages would not the
Irish enjoy if they possessed their own country? A domestic parliament
would encourage Irish manufactures. The linen trade, and the woollen
would be spreading amongst you. An Irish parliament would foster Irish
commerce, and protect Irish agriculture. The labourer, the artizan, and
the shopkeeper would be all benefited by the repeal of the union; but if I
were to describe all the blessings that it would confer I would detain you
here crowding on each other's back until morning before I would be done
(laughter). In the first place, I ask did you ever hear of the tithe rent
charge (groans). Are you satisfied to be paying parsons who do not pray
for you (no, no). It is time, therefore, that they should be put an end to
(hear, hear). The people of England do not pay for the church of the minority.
A Voice. No, nor the people of Scotland either.
You are quite right, though I think I heard the remark before (laughter). But carry home my words with you, and tell them to your neighbours.
I tell you the people of Ireland will not be much longer paying them (hear,
hear, and cheers). I next want to get rid of the poor rates (cheers). England does charity in the way a person will throw a bone to a dog, by slash-
ing it in between his teeth (hear, hear). That is the poor law charity, the
charity of the commissioners and assistant-commissioners, and all concerned under them except the poor themselves, and when they do give re-

lief they take up the poor as if they were criminals, or as if poverty were
a crime to be punished by perpetual imprisonment (hear and cheers). ...
I know it will be said that I want to leave the poor destitute. I do not want
to do any such thing. Would I not have the tithe rent-charge and the ecclesiastical revenues to apply for their relief? And would I not with their aid
be able to maintain hospitals for the sick, the lame, the impotent, the aged,
and all those who are real objects of charity, and for whom the doors would
be open at every hour of the day and during a part of the night, so that any-
body who did not like to remain might go out when they liked (hear, hear,
and cheers)? I would thus do you two pieces of service by the repeal of the
Union. I would relieve the poor without the imposition of poor rates, and
I would prevent you from paying any clergy but your own (loud cheers). I
should not have used the word prevent, because if any of you wished to pay
both you might do it if you pleased (laughter). I often asked protestants
how would they like to pay for the support of the catholic clergy by force,
and they always said they would not like it at all; and why should the catholics like it one bit the better (hear)? Cobbett had a phrase for it. He used
to say 'what's sauce for the goose is sauce for the gander,' (laughter).
The next thing that the repeal would abolish is the grand jury cess (cheers).
I believe it grinds some of you (cries of 'It does so'). There is not a more
iniquitous tax in the world, for it comes on the occupier instead of on the
country at large. Give me the repeal, and the national treasury will pay
for the making and repairing of all the roads, bridges, and public buildings;
and instead of the poor farmers and occupiers paying the money themselves,
it will come from the treasury, and would go in giving employment to those
who now have to pay it (hear, hear). I will tell you another thing I want to
do. I want that every head of a family, every married man and every
householder should have a right to vote for members of parliament. They
say that I would have an interest in that, because I would then have more
votes; but my anser is, if I would it is because the people know I am acting
honestly by them, and everybody else who does the same will be equally
supported. The landlords now persecute those who vote differently from
their wishes, but I would institute the ballot-box. Every married man
should have a vote, and any blackguard who could not get a wife anywhere
I would not pity him to be without the vote (cheers and laughter). The
good landlord would then be sure to be supported by his tenants; but if he
were a scoundrel, whether he was a catholic, protestant, or a presbyterian, he would deserve to be turned out (hear, hear). If he was serving no-
tices to quit, or holding up his head in the street, and not looking his tenants in the face and speaking to them, or if he was a man who would not
salute their wives and children as he passed them, or if, when he sat upon
the bench, he was always fining, fining, fining (loud laughter), the tenant
would always have the advantage of using the ballot-box against that fellow
(hear, hear, and cheers). The next advantage is one that does not much
concern the majority of you. It is the giving the management of their own
affairs to the inhabitants of towns, instead of their having the miserable

municipal reform that they now possess; but I will trouble you farther with
that. You know that the landlords have duties as well as rights, and I
would establish the fixity of tenure (loud cheers) to remind them of these
duties. I will tell you what my plan is, and you can consider it among
yourselves. My plan is that no landlord could recover rent unless he made
a lease for twenty-one years to the tenant -- no lease or no rent say I
(loud cheers). Unless he made a lease, he would have no more business
looking for his rent than a dog would have barking at the moon (cheers and
laughter). It may be said that the landlords would, in that case, put too
high a rent on their lands, but I have a remedy for that too in my plan
(laughter, and cries of 'more power'). At present, if a man goes to register his vote, he must prove on oath what a solvent tenant could pay to his
landlord for his holding, and in the same manner I would give the tenant an
opportunity of proving what a solvent tenant ought to give for his land, in
order to fix the amount of rent he would have to pay (cheers). I would give
the poor man the benefit of a trial by jury in such case, so that it would be
impossible for a landlord to get more than the fair value of his land. It
may be said that the poor man would be turned out of his holding at the expiration of his lease, and his land given to another, but I have a cure for
that also (cheers). I would allow the tenant by law every year to register,
as he can now register trees that he plants, all the improvements that he
makes on his holding, and if the landlord did not pay him the full value of
these improvements, he could not turn him out, but would be obliged to
give him a new holding. Every tenant would be then building a better house
for his pigs than he now inhabits himself, as he would be sure to get every
farthing he laid out on his holding before he could be deprived of possession
at the end of his lease (hear, hear, and cheers). Is it not, I ask you, worth
while to look for a repeal of the union for that alone(cheers)? Would it not
do more to produce happiness and prosperity in the country, and put an end
to the horrible wholesale murders of the landlords who now send their tenants to die by twenties in the ditches, and the fearful retaliations, by assassination, that so frequently take place on the other side (hear). But that
is not all. Every year since the Union nine millions of money has been
sent out of Ireland, after being raised from the produce of the soil (cries
of 'Oh, murder, murder'). It is no wonder you should cry 'murder' for
there is no country in the world where such a system would exist that must
not be poor. The only countries except Ireland where anything like it oc-
curs are Sicily and Sardinia, and both of these, from having absentee landlords, are miserably poor. There is not, however, a country in the world
so impoverished as Ireland, where it has been found that there are
2,300,000 persons in a state of destitution every year. Lord Eliot the
other day gave a proof of that, for he had to admit that out of 83,000 poor
rate payers, 44,000 were rated under £5. For the last ten years no less
than ninety millions have been drawn out of Ireland, but if we get the Union
there will be ninety millions spent in Ireland that would otherwise be taken
from her (hear, hear, and cheers). This will leave an average of £75,000

a month, or £125,000 a week of six days, to be spent in wages and in giving employment to the people (cheers). I have all this within my grasp if the people join me. Now, what is there in all this that Wellington should stammer at in his old age, and that Peel should bluster, and get very angry about it (groans). Do not take the trouble of groaning him (renewed groans). I suppose you groan not so much to dispute with what I ask you as because you do not find it a grouble but a pleasure to groan him. They say we want separation from England, but what I want is to prevent separation taking place, and there is not a man in existence more loyally attached than I am to the Queen -- God bless her. The present state of Ireland is nearly unendurable, and if the people of Ireland had not some person like me to lead them in the paths of peace and constitutional exertion, I am afraid of the result (hear). While I live I will stand by the throne (hear, hear). But what motive could we have to separate if we obtain all those blessings and advantages I have been enumerating? They would all serve as solid golden linke of connexion with England. But I would be glad to know what good did the Union do (hear, hear)? What I want you to do is, for every one of you to join me in looking for Repeal. As many of you as are willing to do so let them hold up their hands (here every person in the immense assemblage raised his hands aloft amidst loud and continued cheers). I see you have ready hands, and I know you have stout hearts too. But what do I want you to do? Is it to turn out into battle or war (cries of no, no)? Is it to commit riot or crime (cries of no, no)? Remember 'whoever commits a crime gives strength to the enemy' (hear, hear, and cheers). ... I want you to do nothing that is not open and legal, but if the people unite with me and follow my advice it is impossible not to get the Repeal (loud cheers and cries of 'we will'). And our country deserves that we should exert ourselves for her. Other countries changed their religious opinions at the fantasy of their governors, but Ireland is the only country that for centuries set her governors at defiance, and she is also the only country that was converted to christianity in the short space of four years (hear, hear, hear) ....

But nothing could be more true, that there was no pursuit of Roman catholic interests as opposed to protestant, and that the object in view was to benefit the whole nation; and because it was a national movement it should never be abandoned until justice was done to the nation (loud cheers). Even their enemies should admit the progress they had made; and let him have but three millions of Repealers, and then he would make his arrangements for obtaining Repeal. He would have the Repealers send up three hundred gentlemen, chosen from various parts of the country, each entrusted with £100, that would be £30,000. They should meet in Dublin to consult upon the best means of obtaining legislative independence. They would not leave Dublin till they would agree to an act of parliament to establish a domestic legislature, household suffrage, vote by ballot, fixity of tenure, and a law against absentees having estates in the country. Many estates would then be sold, in lots and purchased by those who would become small proprietors; and it was a fact well ascertained that in proportion as the owners in fee were numerous in any country, so in proportion were the people prosperous (her, hear). It was truly said by Mr. Martin, their chairman, that if they had their own parliament, taxation would be diminished to almost nothing -- for in five or six years they would be able to pay off their portion of the national debt -- the duty upon every excise-able article would be reduced -- they would have a pound of tea for little more than was now paid for a couple of ounces, and a pound of sugar at the price of a quarter of a pound, the duty on tobacco would be reduced, so that there was not an old woman in the country who might not have her pipe lighted from morning to night if she pleased (laughter). . . . .

THOMAS FRANCIS MEAGHER ON THE USE OF PHYSICAL FORCE, DUBLIN, JULY 28, 1846

Source: The Nation, August 1, 1846.

I will commence as my friend Mr. Mitchel concluded, by an allusion to the whigs (hear, hear). I fully concur with my friend that the "most comprehensive measures" which the whig minister may propose, and the English parliament may adopt will fail to lift this country up to that position which she has the right to occupy, and the power to maintain (cheers). A whig minister, I admit, may improve the province, he will not restore the nation. Franchises, "equal laws," tenant compensation bills, "liberal appointments," in a word "full justice" as they say, may ameliorate, they will not exalt (cheers). They may meet the necessities, they will not call forth the abilities of the country. The errors of the past may be repaired. The hopes of the future will not be fulfilled .... From the stateliest mansion down to the poorest cottage in the land, the inactivity, the meanness, the debasement, which provincialism engenders will be perceptible. These are not the crude sentiments of youth, though the mere commercial politician who has deduced his ideas of self-government from the table of imports and exports may satirize them as such ....

Voter's books and reports, these are the only weapons we can employ (hear). Therefore, my lord, I do advocate the peaceful policy of this association (cheers). If that policy be pursued with truth, with courage, with stern determination of purpose, I do firmly believe that it will succeed (loud and enthusiastic cheers). But, my lord, I dissented from the resolutions in question for other reasons (hear, hear).....I dissented from these resolutions, for I felt that by assenting to them I should have pledged myself to the unqualified repudiation of physical force in all countries, at all times, and in every circumstance. This I could not do, for my lord, I do not abhor the use of arms in the vindication of national rights (cheers). There are times when arms will alone suffice, and when political ameliorations call for a drop of blood -- (cheers) -- and many thousand drops of blood (enthusiastic cheering and cries of "Oh, Oh"). Opinion I admit will operate against opinion. But, as the hon. member of Kilkenny observed, force must be used against force (cheers and some confusion). The soldier is proof against an argument but he is not proof against the bullet. The man that will listen to reason, let him be reasoned with, but it is the weaponed arm of the patriot that can alone avail against battalioned despotism (loud cheers). Then, my lord, I do not disclaim the use of force as immoral, nor do I believe that it is the truth to say that the God of Heaven withholds His sanction from the use of arms. From the day on which in the valley of Bethulia He nerved the arm of the Jewish girl to smite the drunken tyrant in his tent, down to the hour in which He blessed the insurgent chivalry of the Belgian priests, His Almighty hand has ever been stretched forth from His throne of light, to consecrate the flag of freedom, to bless the patriot's sword (loud and enthusiastic cheering). . Be it for the defence or be it for the assertion of a nation's liberty, I look upon the sword as a sacred weapon ("No, No" from the Rev. Mr. Hopkins). And if my lord it has sometimes reddened the shroud of the oppressor, like the annointed rod of the high priest, it has other times blossomed into flowers to deck the freeman's brow (vehement applause). Abhor the sword and stigmatize the sword? No, my lord, for in the cragged passes of the Tyrol it cut in pieces the banner of the Bavarian, and won an immortality for the peasant of Innsbruck (hear). Abhor the sword and stigmatize the sword? No, my lord, for at its blow a giant nation sprung up from the waters of the far Atlantic, and by its redeeming magic the fettered colony became a daring free republic. Abhor the sword and stigmatize the sword? No, my lord, for it scourged the Dutch marauders out of the fine old towns of Belgium, back into their own phlegmatic swamps -- (cheers) -- and knocked their flag, and laws, and sceptre, and bayonets, into the sluggish waters of the Scheldt (enthusiastic cheers).

A VIEW OF THE FAMINE, 1847

Source: Isaac Butt, "Ireland's Calamity," <u>Dublin</u> <u>University</u> <u>Magazine</u>, vol. XIII, pp. 100-109 (April, 1847).

IRELAND is now, in one sense, in the midst, in another sense, we fear, in the beginning of a calamity, the like of which the world has never seen. Four millions of people, the majority of whom were always upon the verge of utter destitution, have been suddenly deprived of the sole article of their ordinary food. Without any of the ordinary channels of commercial intercourse, by which such a loss could be supplied, the country has had no means of replacing the withdrawal of this perished subsistence, and the consequence has been, that in a country that is called civilized, under the protection of the mightiest monarchy upon earth, and almost within a day's communication of the capital of the greatest and richest empire in the world, thousands of our fellow-creatures are each day dying of starvation, and the wasted corpses of many left unburied in their miserable hovels, to be devoured by the hungry swine; or to escape this profanation, only to diffuse among the living the malaria of pestilence and death.

As we proceed, we trust it will be seen that we have no inclination either to exaggerate or unnecessarily to alarm; but it were criminal to disguise the extent of the calamity, or to shrink from telling all the hideous truth. We must presume that there are none of our readers to whom the evidences upon which this statement rests are not familiar, in the appalling narratives that have filled the journals of the empire for the last few months. It is long since the coroners gave over in despair the task of holding inquests upon the bodies of those whom starvation had stricken down. Our journals have become unable to record, our people to communicate, the deaths which in some districts result from insufficient food. "Death by starvation" has ceased to be an article of news, and day by day multitudes of our population are swept down into the pit -- literally into the pit -- in which the victims of the famine are interred.

We will not take up our space by repeating the testimonies, which prove incontestably that this is no exaggeration. It is not, perhaps, the least appalling feature of this calamity, that it is difficult, if not impossible, to obtain accurate information upon the extent of devastation that has already taken place. Nearly a month ago the deaths that had resulted in one shape or other from starvation were estimated at 240,000. Long before the same period, the deaths that were occurring each day in Ireland beyond those of the same period in the preceding year, were estimated at 1,000 -- 1,000 each day -- a number we apprehend below the truth. In many of the workhouses deaths occurred in numbers that would lead to a much greater estimate of the loss of life in the entire country. In one electoral poor-law division of the county Cork -- one not within the fatal district of Schull or Skibbereen -- out of a population of 16,000, the deaths in the early part of March were averaging 70 a day, a rate of mortality that would sweep away the entire population in about eight months.

There are parts of Mayo, Galway, and Sligo, in which the deaths were nearly in the same proportion. It is impossible, however, to form more than an approximation to the real extent of the calamity. . . .

In the autumn of 1845, it was discovered that a disease had attacked the potato in Ireland, and in several other parts of the world. Of the actual existence of such a disease there was no doubt. Its extent was, like most questions in Ireland, made a party one -- and, we grieve to say, the Tory party were in the wrong. Some of the journals in Ireland, supposed most to represent the aristocracy, persisted in vigorously denying the existence of any failure to more than a very partial extent. The question of the corn laws, then pending, gave this question an imperial interest. The potato famine in Ireland was represented as the invention of the agitators on either side of the water. So far was party feeling carried, that the conservative mayor of Liverpool, honestly, we are sure, refused to convene a meeting for the relief of Irish distress -- A committee which sat at the Mansion House, in Dublin, and first declared their belief in the approach of an overwhelming calamity, were stigmatised as deluding the public with a false alarm. Men's politics determined their belief. To profess belief in the fact of the existence of a formidable potato blight, was as sure a method of being branded as a radical, as to propose to destroy the Church.

Thus in the very outset of this sore trial did Ireland encounter that which has ever been her bitterest curse -- that questions of fact are made party questions, and the belief or disbelief of matters of fact is regulated in each man's mind, not by the real state of the case, but by his own political prejudices or opinions.

Sir Robert Peel was then at the head of affairs, and the ministry certainly foresaw the coming calamity. Inquiries were made as to the substance that would be the best and cheapest substitute for the potato. Indian corn was adopted, and without any public excitement on the subject, orders were given by the government for the importation of Indian corn to the amount of £1,000,000. This timely precaution, and the subsequent judicious distribution of this store, had the effect of bringing the people through the winter that closed the year 1845, without exposing them to any very severe privations. Arrangements were made by the government for the supply of provisions in biscuit and rice, to a much greater extent, if needed. However men may differ as to the merits of Sir Robert Peel as a politician, whatever estimate may be formed of his measures, it is impossible to deny that for the limited distress that existed consequent upon the partial failure of the potato crop of 1845, provision was made with the most consummate skill -- at least with the most complete success. Uninfluenced by party representations, the minister had evidently accurately informed himself of the nature of the calamity, and clearly foresaw its extent. That he erred in fixing too early a period for its full realization, subsequent events have proved; but this was an error on the right side; and all that Sir Robert Peel predicted of the fearful extent of calamity which he anticipated in the summer of 1846, has been more than realized in the spring of 1847. . . . . .

The destruction of the potato crop entailed a double misery upon the poor. It destroyed their food, and at the same time it took from them their income. Let the corn of England fail, and you have indeed the distress among her population that a scarcity of the means of subsistence will occasion, but the capacity of the great mass of the people to purchase that subsistence, were it offered at the accustomed price, is left unimpaired. Far different, however, was the effect of the withering of the potato gardens and the con-acres of Ireland. The poor man's store was altogether gone -- a purchaser of his provisions he never had been -- the means of purchasing he never had.

The new year opened gloomily on Ireland. By this time the appalling extent of the calamity, and the inefficiency of the measures adopted to meet it, were, at least, partially understood. . . . Men who have hated democracy all their lives, began seriously to reflect whether the people had influence enough upon a Parliament in which their sufferings were so little heeded. Irishmen, too, began to feel that they were legislated for by men ignorant of the condition and circumstances of their country.

EDITORIAL IN THE NATION, JULY 22, 1848
ON THE EVE OF THE YOUNG IRELAND INSURRECTION

THE HOUR OF DESTINY

The last plank has now, indeed, been shivered, to which we clung with such despairing faith. The last drop added to the full cup of insult and misery, it has overflowed. Men of Ireland, the hour of trial and deliverance has at last been struck by Providence. Only contemplate all that God, humanity, and your outraged country demand of you, and then resolutely dare, heroically conquer, or bravely die. What have you to fear? Nothing in Heaven, for you are justified before God. You may kneel by your lifted battle flag and call upon Him to witness how you have patiently endured every wrong, suffered, unrevenged, every infamy, and sought redress only with streaming eyes and clasped hands, and passionate prayers for Justice!

Justice! That cry has gone up to Heaven and entered into the ears of the Lord of Sabaoth, but it could not move the hearts of men. We appeal to God, then, on the day of battle. We claim His vengeance for our wrongs, for has He not said, "Vengeance is mine, saith the Lord?"

Do you fear the judgement of men? Look round the Earth -- every nation cheers you on with words of hope, and sympathy, and encouragement. Uplift your battle flag, and from the two hemispheres and from across the two oceans, not words alone but brave hearts and armed hands will come to aid you.

Ireland! Ireland! It is no petty insurrection, no local quarrel, no party triumph that summons you to the field. The destinies of the world -- the advancement of the human race -- depends now upon your courage and success, for if you have courage, success must follow. Tyranny, and despotism, and injustice, and bigotry are gathering together the chains that have been flung off by every other nation in Europe, and are striving to bind them upon us -- the ancient, brave, free Irish people. It is a hold war to which we are called -- a war against all that is opposed to justice, and happiness, and freedom. Conquer, and tyranny is subdued forever.

It is a death struggle now between the oppressor and the slave -- between the murderer and his victim. Strike! Strike! Another instant and his foot will be upon your neck -- his dagger at your heart. Will he listen to your prayers? Will he melt at your tears? God help us! We have looked to Heaven and the Earth and asked, "Is there no way to save Ireland but by this dark path?" We have taken counsel of Misery, and Famine, and Plague, and said, "Will ye plead for us?" Will not Horror grant what Justice denies? But they die! -- They die! The strong men, and the mothers and the pale children, down they fall, thousands upon thousands -- a death ruin of human corpses upon the earth, and their groans vibrate with a fearful dissonance through the country, and their death-wail shrieks along the universe, but no pity dims the stern eye of the murderer who watches their agonies.

Then rose a band of martyrs, and they stood between the living and the dead, and preached the <u>truth,</u> such as the world has known from the beginning, only they preached it more eloquently, for they were young and gifted, and genius burned in their eyes, and patriotism in their hears -- and God had filled these noble young spirits with a lofty enthusiasm for the devinest purpose -- the redemption of their country. But what care they for genius or virtue or patriotism, those iron machines called Governments who "grind down men's bones to a pale unanimity?" So they trembled at the voices of these young preachers, and strove to crush them by cunning and ingenious tortures that made life more terrible even than death, and soon in there were noble hearts writhing in prison, and proud hearts beating in ignominious exile; and now with the groans of the dying there went up from our fated land the shrieks of despairing mothers, and the weeping of young wives, desolate by their lonely hearth, and the bewildered cries of orphaned children when they heard they had no father.

What then? Is there no hope? Will ye drag on a wretched existence, degraded in the eyes of Europe -- making Ireland a by-word among the nations? Will ye suffer these things so that your children may rise up in after years and say -- Was it thus and thus when ye were young men, and ye never lifted your right arms to prevent it? Did ye sell not only the lives of your brothers but the honour of your country? Have ye left nothing but a heritage of shame?

No! God has not utterly forsaken us. He has left us <u>one</u> path, but one. That path is broad and clear, and open to us <u>now</u>. There <u>is no other</u>. You must march on it, or the ruin of your country, the death of the living, and the vengeance of the unavenged dead will lie upon your soul .... Rise then, men of Ireland, since Providence so wills it. Rise in your cities and your fields, on your hills, in your valleys, by your dark mountain passes, by your rivers and lakes and ocean-washed shores. Rise as a <u>nation.</u> England has dissevered the bond of allegiance. Rise, not now to demand justice from a foreign kingdom, but to make Ireland an independent kingdom forever ....

You look round upon a land -- it is your land -- trodden down and trampled and devastated, and on a persecuted, despairing people. It is your right arm must raise up that land -- must make her again beautiful and stately and rich in blessings. Elevate that despairing people, and make them free and happy, but teach them to be majestic in their force, generous in their clemency, noble in their triumph.

It is a holy mission. Holy must be your motives and your acts if you would fulfill it. Act as if your soul's salvation hung on each deed, it will; for we stand already within the shadows of eternity. For us is the combat, but not for us, perhaps, the triumph. Many a noble heart will lie cold, many a throbbing pulse will be stilled ere the day of Victory will come. It is a solemn though that now is the hour of destiny, when the fetters of seven centuries may at last be broken, and by you, men of this generation -- by you, men of Ireland. You are God's instruments; many of you must be freedom's martyrs. Oh! be worthy of the name, and as you act as men, as patriots, and as Christians, so will the blessing rest upon your head when you lat it down, a sacrifice for Ireland, upon the red battle-field.

RESOLUTIONS OF THE TENANT-RIGHT CONFERENCE OF 1850

Source: The Freeman's Journal, August 7, 1850

Section I

1. That a fair valuation of rent between landlord and tenant in Ireland is indispensible.

2. That the tenant shall not be disturbed in his possession so long as he pays the rent fixed by the proposed law.

3. That the tenant shall have a right to sell his interest, with all its incidents, at the highest market value.

4. That where the rent has been fixed by valuation, no rent beyond the valued rent shall be recoverable by any process of law.

5. That cases of minors and other exceptional cases be considered hereafter in any measure to be introduced into parliament.

6. That it be an instruction to the league to take into consideration, at the earliest possible period, the condition of farm labourers, and suggest some measure for their permanent protection and improvement, in connection with the arrangement of the question between landlord and tenant.

Section II

1. That an equitable valuation of land for rent should divide between the landlord and the tenant the net profits of cultivation, in the same way as the profits would be divided between the partners in any other business where one of them is a dormant partner and the other the working capitalist who take upon him the whole risk.

2. That nothing shall be included in the valuation or paid under the valuation to the landlord on account of improvements made by the tenant in possession, or those under whom he claims, unless these have been paid for by the landlord in reduced rent or in some other way.

3. That if the landlord shall at any time have made improvements either when the land is in his own occupation, or with the consent of the tenant in occupation, or if the landlord shall have brought the tenant's improvements, the landlord shall have the right, on letting the same to a new tenant, or on giving notice to the tenant in possession, to have such improvements valued for the purpose of adding to the rent.

4. That wherever in Ulster, or elsewhere, tenant-right custom has prevailed, the value of such right, according to the local custom, shall be considered in all respects as an improvement made by the tenant, and allowed for accordingly in valuing the rent.

5. That where land is held under lease, the lease shall not be

disturbed unless at the request of the lessee or his assigns in possession; and if on such requests the rent be altered by the valuators, the tenant shall hold in future at the altered rent.

6.   That the valuation when once made, shall be permanent.

7.   That every seven years there may and shall be a re-adjustment of the rent payable under the valuation, according to the rise or fall of the prices of agricultural produce, when the rise in prices be manifestly occasioned by the deficiency of the crops.

Section III

1.   That the valuation shall be made by tribunals which shall unite as far as possible the advantages of <u>impartiality</u> between landlord and tenant, cheapness, accessibility, and <u>nomination</u> by the parties interested.

2.   That these advantages may be secured to a reasonable degree -- first by local tribunals, consisting of two valuators, one appointed by the landed proprietors and the other by the tenant farmers of the poor law union; secondly by having valuators bound to value according to instructions embodied in the law; and thirdly by having attached to each local tribunal a registrar or secretary, whose duty it shall be to register all the proceedings of the valuators, and keep them informed and reminded of the requirements of the instructions under which they act.

Rules of the League

1.   That an association to be called The Irish Tenant League, be formed on the principles, and subject to the rules hereafter expressed; and that such League be hereby established accordingly.

2.   That the sole objects of the Tenant League are to protect the tenant, and to procure a good landlord-and-tenant law by the legal co-operation of persons of all classes and of all opinions on other subjects.

BRITISH REACTION TO THE RISE
OF THE FENIAN BROTHERHOOD, 1859-67

Source: <u>The Times</u> (London) - (1) April 1, 1859; (2) September 18, September 22, 1865; (3) December 14, December 16, 1867. The reference is to the explosion of a Fenian bomb at Clerkenwell on December 13.

...The return, after so many years intermission, to Riband Societies, to a course of agrarian crime, to treasonable oaths and secret conspiracies, is certainly a bitter disappointment to our bright and sanguine hopes. We had dreamt of another future for Ireland, and can scarcely prevail upon ourselves to awake and look in the face our present disappointments -- to admit how deeprooted are the evils with which we have striven to contend, and how ill the race in whose destiny we are so deeply interested profits by the opportunities of prosperity or the teaching of adversity ... If the Irish cannot be content with their lot, the fault we are now convinced is theirs, not ours ... (1)

...Their enterprise may not be the wickedest, but, so far as we can judge, it is by far the wildest, except perhaps Smith O'Brien's, that has yet been planned by Irish agitators. Almost the only thing we know for certain about them is that the establishment of an Irish Republic is one of their main objects. A more extravagant and chimerical idea never entered the head of an Irishman ... Is there any people under the sun more unfitted for a Republican form of Government than the Irish? Is there any character so deficient in those political virtues which are the life of Republics as the Celtic? ... The truth is that Fenianism has not and could not have sprung up spontaneously on Irish soil. It is entirely of exoltic growth, an importation from America, and entirely out of harmony with real Irish sentiment .... (2)

...A crime of unexampled atrocity has been committed in the midst of London ... the slaughter of a number of innocent people; the burning and mangling of women and helpless infants, the destruction of poor men's homes and poor men's property .... As to the Fenian conspiracy itself, it must be evident that the time is past for clemency and forbearance. With traitors and assassins there can be but one course.
...The Fenians have cast the glare of a great moral crime upon the debatable ground which separates us, and we can no longer hesitate in which direction to advance. No man worthy of the name will venture to adduce political discontent in palliation of such an outrage ... We are confronted by a gang of reckless criminals, who respect no laws, human or divine ... We must crush them at any cost ..... (3)

FOUNDATION OF THE NATIONAL LAND LEAGUE OF MAYO, 1879

Source: The Freeman's Journal, Agust 18, 1879.

A meeting in connexion with the land agitation in Mayo, ...took place at Castlebar to-day in Daly's Hotel, and was attended by representative delegates from all parts of the county ... Mr. Michael Davitt read a document embodying the rules and objects of the proposed association.

This body shall be known as The National Land League of Mayo, and shall consist of farmers and others, who will agree to labour for the objects here set forth, and subscribe to the conditions of membership, principles, and rules specified below ---

Objects: The objects for which this body is organized are --

1. To watch over the interests of the people it represents; and protect the same, as far as may be in its power to do so, from an unjust or capricious exercise of power or privilege on the part of landlords or any other class in the community.

2. To resort to every means compatible with justice, morality, and right reason which shall not clash defiantly with the constitution upheld by the power of the British empire in this country, for the abolition of the present land laws of Ireland, and the substitution in their place of such a system as shall be in accord with the social rights and necessities of our people, the traditions and moral sentiments of our race, and which the contentment and prosperity of our country imperatively demand.

3. Pending a final and satisfactory settlement of the land question, the duty of this body will be to expose the injustice, wrong, or injury which may be inflicted upon any farmer in Mayo, either by rack-renting, eviction, or other arbitrary exercise of power which the existing laws enables the landlords to exercise over their tenantry, by giving all such arbitrary acts the widest possible publicity, and meeting their perpetration with all the opposition which the laws for the preservation of the peace will permit of. In furtherance of which the following plan will be adopted: -- a. Returns to be obtained, printed, and circulated, of the number of landlords in this county; the amount of acreage in possession of same, and the means by which such land was obtained; farms let by each, with the conditions under which they are held by their tenants and excess of rent paid by same over the government valuation. b. To publish by placard, or otherwise, notice of contemplated evictions for non-payment of exorbitatnt rent, or other unjust cause, and the convening of a public meeting if deemed necessary or expedient, as near the scene of such evictions, as circumstances will allow, and on the day fixed upon for the same. c. The publication of a list of evictions carried out, together with cases of rack-renting, giving full particulars of same, names of landlords, agents, etc., concerned, and number of people evicted by such acts. d. The publication of the names of all per-

sons who shall rent or occupy land or farms, from which others have been dispossessed for non-payment of exorbitant rents, or who shall offer a higher rent for land or farms than that paid by the previous occupier. e. The publication of reductions of rent, and acts of justice or kindness performed by landlords in the county.

4. This body to undertake the defence of such of its members, or those of local clubs affiliated with it, who may be required to resist by law the actions of landlords or their agents, who may purpose doing them injury, wrong, or injustice in connexion with their land or farms.

5. To render assistance when possible to such farmer-members as may be evicted or otherwise wronged by landlords or their agents.

6. To undertake the organizing of local clubs or difence associations in the baronies, towns, and parishes of this county, the holding of public meetins and demonstrations on the land question, and the printing of pamphlets on that and other subjects for the information of the farming classes.

7. And finally to act as a vigilance committee in Mayo, note the conduct of its grand jury, poor law guardians, town commissioners, and members of parliament and pronounce on the manner in which their respective functions are performed wherever the interests social or political, of the people represented by this club renders it expedient to do so.

Conditions of membership: 1. To be a member of any local club or defence association in the county, and be selected by such club or association to represent the same on the central or county association. 2. A desire to co-operate in the carrying out of the foregoing objects and subscribing to the principles here enunciated with the view of propagating the same and labouring for their successful application in Ireland will qualify non-representative farmers or others for membership of this body, subject to the subscription and rules laid down for same. 3. To pay any sum not under five shillings a year towards the carrying out of the foregoing objects and the end for which this body is created -- the obtaining of the soil of Ireland for the people of Ireland who cultivate it.

Declaration of principles. The land of Ireland belongs to the people of Ireland, to be held and cultivated for the sustenance of those whom God decreed to be the inhabitants thereof. Land being created to supply the necessities of existence, those who cultivate it to that end have a higher claim to its absolute possession than those who make it an article of barter to be used or disposed of for purposes of profit or pleasure. The end for which the land of a cou ntry is created requires an equitable distribution of the same among the people who are to live upon the fruits of their labour in its cultivation. Any restriction, therefore, upon such a distribution by a feudal land system embodying the laws of primogeniture and entail, the amassing of large estates, the claiming of proprietorship under penal obligations from occupiers, and preventing the same from developing the full resources of the land, must necessarily be opposed to the Divine purpose for which it was created, and to the social rights, security, and happiness of the people.

"Before the conquest the Irish people knew nothing of absolute property in land. The land virtually belonged to the entire sept, the chief was little more than the managing member of the association. The feudal idea, which views all rights as emanating from a head landlord, came with the conquest, was associated with foreign dominion, and has never to this day been recognized by the moral sentiments of the people. Originally the offspring, not of industry, but of spoilation, the right has not been allowed to purify itself by protracted possession, but has passed from the original spoilators to others by a series of fresh spoilations, so as to be always connected with the latest and most odious oppression of foreign invaders. In the moral feelings of the Irish people, the right to hold the land goes, as it did in the beginning, with the right to till it." These were the words of John Stuart Mill,. the English political economist.

The landlord system which an alien government has imposed upon our country in the place of that which recognized no intermediate ownership between the cultivator of the soil and the state has reduced Ireland to a degree of poverty and social misery incompatible with the natural productiveness of its land and the progressive prosperity of other civilized nations.

The area of Ireland and the natural wealth of its soil is capable of supporting from twelve to twenty millions of inhabitants, if restrictive land laws did not operate against the full development of the country's resources and the unfettered cultivation of the land. Yet a population of 8,000,000 previous to the year 1847 was reduced by death, starvation and exile, consequent upon an artificial famine and continued impoverishment to little over 5,000,000 at the present day. Decreased population with its concomitant absorption of small-holdings into large estates has produced no beneficial changes in the condition of the existent farming classes who are compelled by the coercion of necessity in the absence of manufacturing industry to the acceptance of a non-alternative bargain in the shape of exorbitant rent in order to obtain the use of the soil. The dread of eviction or rackrenting must necessarily operate against that expenditure of labour and enterprise in the cultivation of the land and improvement of farm dwellings and premises which follow in every country where the fruits of the people's industry is protected by the state; hence the soil of Ireland is worse and less cultivated, and the living and habitations of its agricultural classes more wretched than in any country in the civilized world. Over 6,000,000 acres of Irish land is owned by less than 300 individuals, twelve of whom are in possession of 1,297,888 acres between them, while 5,000,000 of the Irish people own not a solitary acre. For the protection of the proprietorial rights of the few thousand landlords in the country a standing army of semi-military police is maintained which the landless millions have to support, while the conduct of the landocracy in the exercise of its legal privileges occasions almost all the evils under which our people suffer.

Thus the rights of the soil cultivators, their security from arbitrary disturbance and incentives to social advancement, together with the general well-being, peace, and prosperity of the people at large are sacrificed for

the benefit of a class insignificant in numbers, and of least account in all
that goes towards the maintenance of a country, but which by the aid of existing land laws extracts some twenty million pounds annually from the soil
of Ireland without conferring any single benefit in return on the same or
the people by whose industry it is produced.

If the land in the possession of 744 landlords in this country were divided into 20-acre farms it would support in ease and comparative independence over two millions and a half of our people.

To substitute for such an unjust and anomalous system as the present
land code -- one that would show an equal protection and solicitude for the
social rights and well-being of the labouring millions as that shown for
those of the wealthy but non-operative few -- is the principle upon which
enlightened statesmanship aims at following in modern times to meet the
growing necessitites of that popular intelligence and awakening civilization
which demands the sweeping away of those feudal laws opposed to the social progress and ideas of the age. Sacrificing the interests of the few to t
the welfare of the many by the abolition of feudal land codes, has laid the
foundation of solid governments and secured the contentment of peoples in
most European countries. The interests of the landlords of Ireland are
pecuniary and can be compensated, but the interests of the people of Ireland, dependant upon the produce of the soil, is their very existence. In
denouncing the existing land laws and demanding in their place such a system as will recognize and establish the cultivator of the said soil as its
proprietor, we neither purpose nor demand the confiscation of the interest
which the landlords now hold in the land, but ask that compensation be giv-
en them for loss of said rights when the state for the peace, benefit and
happiness of the people shall decree the abolition of the present system.

We appeal to the farmers of Ireland to be up and doing at once, and
organize themselves forthwith in order that their full strength may be put
forth in behalf of themselves and their country in efforts to obtain what has
brought security and comparative plenty to the farming classes of continen-
tal countries. Without an evidence of earnestness and practical determination being shown now by the farmers of Ireland and their friends in a demand for a small proprietary which alone can fully satisfy the Irish people
or finally settle the great land question of the country, the tribunal of public opinion will neither credit the urgent necessity for such a change nor
lend its influence in ameliorating the condition or redressing the social and
political wrongs of which we complain. Let us remember, in the words of
one of Ireland's greatest sons, that "the land is the fund whence we all ultimately draw; and if the terms on which the land is cultivated be unfair --
if the agricultural system of a country be unsound, then the entire structure
is rotten and will inevitably come down. Let us never forget that mere appeals to the public to encourage native industry in other departments must
be utterly futile so long as the great and paramount native industry of the
farmer is neglected. In vain shall we try to rouse national spirit if the
very men who make the nation sink into paupers before our face. Paupers

have no country, no rights, no duties; and, in short, if we permit the small farmers to be reduced to pauperism -- if we see them compelled to give up their land and throw themselves on public relief, there is an end of Ireland.

The manifesto was unanimously adopted.

PARNELL AND THE LAND WAR: SPEECH AT ENNIS, 1880

Source: <u>The Freeman's Journal</u>, September 20, 1880

     . . . Depend upon it that the measure of the land bill of next session will be the measure of your activity and energy this winter (cheers) -- it will be the measure of your determination not to pay unjust rents -- it will be the measure of your determination to keep a firm grip of your home- steads (cheers). It will be the measure of your determination not to bid for farms from which others have been evicted, and to use the strong force of public opinion to deter any unjust men amongst yourselves -- and there are many such -- from bidding for such farms (hear, hear). If you refuse to pay unjust rents, if you refuse to take farms from which others have been evicted, the land question must be settled, and settled in a way that will be satisfactory to you. It depends, therefore, upon yourselves, and not upon any commission or any government. When you have made this question ripe for settlement then and not till then will it be settled (cheers). It is very nearly ripe already in many parts of Ireland. It is ripe in Mayo, Galway, Roscommon, Sligo, and portions of the county Cork (cheers). But I regret to say that the tenant farmers of the county Clare have been back- ward in organization up to the present time. You must take and band your- selves together in Land Leagues. Every town and village must have its own branch. You must know the circumstances of the holdings and of the tenures of the district over which the League has jurisdiction -- you must see that the principles of the Land League are inculcated, and when you have done this in Clare, then Clare will take her rank with the other active counties, and you will be included in the next land bill brought forward by the government (cheers). Now, what are you to do to a tenant who bids for a farm from which another tenant has been evicted?

     Several voices. Shoot him.

     Mr. Parnell. I think I heard somebody say shoot him(cheers). I wish to point out to you a very much better way -- a more christian and chari- table way, which will give the lost man an opportunity of repenting (laugh- ter, and hear). When a man takes a farm from which another has been evicted you must shun him on the roadside when you meet him -- you must shun him in the streets of the town -- you must shun him in the shop -- you must shun him in the fair-green and in the market place, and even in the place of worship, by leaving him alone, by putting him into a moral Coventry, by isolating him from the rest of his country as if he were the leper of old -- you must show him your detestation of the crime he has committed. If you do this, you may depend on it there will be no man so full of avarice -- so lost to shame -- as to dare the public opinion of all the right-thinking men in the county and transgress your unwritten code of laws. People are very much engaged at present in discussing the way in which the

land question is to be settled, just the same as when a few years ago Irishmen were at each other's throats as to the sort of parliament we would l
have if we got one. I am always thinking it is better first to catch your
hare before you decide how you are going to cook him (laughter). I would
strongly recommend public men not to waste their breath too much in dis-
cussing how the land question is to be settled, but rather to help and encourage the people in making it, as I said just now, ripe for settlement
(applause). When it is ripe for settlement you will probably have your
choice as to how it shall be settled and I said a year ago that the land question would never be settled until the Irish landlords were just as anxious
to have it settled as the Irish tenants (cheers).

A voice. They soon will be.

Mr. Parnell. There are, indeed, so many ways in which it may be
settled that it is almost superfluous to discuss them; but I stand here today to express my opinion that no settlement can be satisfactory or permanent which does not ensure the uprooting of that system of landlordism
which has brought the country three times in a century to famine. The feudal system of land tenure has been tried in almost every European country
and it has been found wanting everywhere; but nowhere has it brought more
exile, produced more suffering, crime and destitution than in Ireland
(cheers). It was abolished in Prussia by transferring the land from the
landlords to the occupying tenants. The landlords were given government
paper as compensation. Let the English government give the landlords
their paper to-morrow as compensation (laughter). We want no money --
not a single penny of money would be necessary. Why, if they gave the
Irish landlords -- the bad section of them -- the four or five millions a
year that they spend on the police and military (groans) in helping them to
collect their rents, that would be a solution of it (cheers), and a very cheap
solution of it. But, perhaps, as with other reforms, they will try a little
patchwork and tinkering for a while until they learn better (hear, hear).
Well, let them patch and tinker if they wish. In my opinion the longer the
landlords wait, the worse the settlement they will get (cheers). Now is
the time for them to settle before the people learn the power of combination. We have been accused of preaching communisitc doctrines when we
told the people not to pay an unjust rent, and the following out of that advice in a few of the Irish counties had shown the English government the
necessity for a radical alteration in the land laws. But how would they like
it if we told the people some day or other not to pay any rent until this question is settled (cheers). We have not told them that yet, and I suppose it
may never be necessary for us to speak in that way (hear). I suppose the
question will be settled peaceably, fairly, and justly to all parties (hear,
hear). If it should not be settled, we cannot continue to allow this mill-
stone to hang round the neck of our country, throttling its industry, and
preventing its progress (cheers). It will be for the consideration of wiser
heads than mine whether, if the landlords continue obdurate, and refuse all
just concessions, we shall not be obliged to tell the people of Ireland to

strike against rent until this question has been settled (cheers). And if the five hundred thousand tenant farmers of Ireland struck against the ten thousand landlords, I would like to see where they would get police and soldiers enough to make them pay (loud cheers).

AN ACT TO FURTHER AMEND THE LAW RELATING TO
THE OCCUPATION AND OWNERSHIP OF LAND IN
IRELAND, AND FOR OTHER PURPOSES
RELATING THERETO, 1881

Source: Public General Acts of the United Kingdom of Great Britain and
Ireland (London, 1881), pp. 139-64.

Be it enacted ... as follows:

1.   The tenant for the time being of every holding, not hereinafter specially excepted from the provions of this act, may sell his tenancy for the
best price that can be got for the same, subject to the following regulations
and subject also to the provisions in this act contained with respect to statutory conditions:

(1) Except with the consent of the landlord, the sale shall be made
to one person only:

(2) The tenant shall give the prescribed notice to the landlord of
his intention to sell his tenancy:

(3) On receiving such notice the landlord may purchase the tenancy for such sum as may be agreed upon, or in the event of disagreement
may be ascertained by the court to be the true value thereof:

(4) Where the tenant shall agree to sell his tenancy to some other
person than the landlord, he shall, upon informing the landlord of the name
of the purchaser, state in writing therewith the consideration agreed to be
given for the tenancy:

(5) If the tenant fails to give the landlord the notice or information required by the foregoing sub-sections, the court may, if it think fit
and that the just interests of the landlord so require, declare the sale to
be void:

(6) Where the tenancy is sold to some other person than the landlord, the landlord may within the prescribed period refuse on reasonable
grounds to accept the purchaser as tenant. In case of dispute the reason-
ableness of the landlord's refusal shall be decided by the court:....

(7) Where the tenancy is subject to any such conditions as are in
this act declared to be statutory conditions, and the sale is made in consequence of proceedings by the landlord for the purpose of recovering possession of the holding by reason of the breach of any of such conditions,
the court shall grant to the landlord out of the purchase moneys payment
of any debt, including arrears of rent, due to him by the tenant ....

(8) Where permanent improvements on a holding have been made
by the landlord or his predecessors in title ... and the landlord ... con-
sents that his property in such improvements shall be sold along with the
tenancy ... the purchase money shall be apportioned by the court as between the landlord's property in such improvements, and the tenancy....

(9) When a tenant sells his tenancy to any person other than the landlord, the landlord may at any time within the prescribed period give notice both to the outgoing tenant and to the purchaser of any sums which he may claim from the outgoing tenant for arrears of rent or other breaches of the contract or conditions of tenancy. And

(a) If the outgoing tenant does not within the prescribed period give notice to the purchaser that he disputes such claims or any of them, the purchaser shall out of the purchase moneys pay the full amount thereof to the landlord; and

(b) If the outgoing tenant disputes such cliams or any of them, the purchaser shall out of the purchase moneys pay to the landlord so much (if any) of such claims as the outgoing tenant admits, and pay the residue of the amount claimed by the landlord into court in the prescribed manner.

Until the purchaser has satisfied the requirements of this subsection, it shall not be obligatory on the landlord to accept the purchaser as his tenant.

(11) A tenant who has sold his tenancy on any occasion of quitting his holding shall not be entitled on the same occasion to receive compensation for either disturbance of improvements; and a tenant who has received compensation for either disturbance or improvements on any occasion of quitting his holding shall not be entitled on the same occasion to sell his tenancy.

(12) The tenant of a holding subject to the Ulster tenant-right custom or to a usage corresponding to the Ulster tenant-right custom may sell his tenancy either in pursuance of that custom or usage, or in pursuance of this section, ...

4.   Where the landlord demands an increase of rent from the tenant of a present tenancy ... or demands an increase of rent from the tenant of a future tenancy beyond the amount fixed at the beginning of such tenancy, then,

(1) Where the tenant accepts such increase, until the expiration of a term of fifteen years from the time when such increase was made (in this act referred to as a statutory term) such tenancy shall (if it so long continues to subsist) be deemed to be a tenancy subject to statutory conditions, with such incidents during the continuance of the said term as are in this act in that behalf mentioned.

(2) Where the tenant of any future tenancy does not accept such increase and sells his tenancy, the same shall be sold subject to the increased rent, and in addition to the price paid for the tenancy, he shall be entitled to receive from his landlord the amount (if any) by which the court may, on the application of the landlord or tenant, decide the selling value of his tenancy to have been depreciated below the amount which would have been such selling value if the rent had been a fair rent, ...

(3) Where the tenant does not accept such increase and is compelled to quit the tenancy by or in pursuance of a notice to quit, but does not sell the tenancy, he shall be entitled to claim compensation as in

the case of disturbance by the landlord.

(4) The tenant of a present tenancy may in place of accepting or declining such increase apply to the court in manner hereafter in this act mentioned to have the rent fixed.

5.   A tenant shall not, during the continuance of a statutory term in his tenancy, be compelled to pay a higher rent than the rent payable at the commencement of such term, and shall not be compelled to quit the holding of which he is tenant except in consequence of the breach of some one or more of the conditions following (in this act referred to as statutory conditions), that is to say,

(1) The tenant shall pay his rent at the appointed time.

(2) The tenant shall not, to the prejudice of the interest of the landlord in the holding, commit persistent waste...

(3) The tenant shall not, without the consent of his landlord in writing, subdivide his holding or sub-let the same..... Agistment or the letting of land for the purpose of temporary depasturage, or the letting in conacre of land for the purpose of its being solely used ... for the growing of potatoes or other green crops, the land being properly manured, shall not be deemed a sub-letting for the purposes of this act.

(5) The landlord, or any person or persons authorized by him in that behalf (he or they making reasonable amends and satisfaction for any damage to be done or occasioned thereby), shall have the right to enter upon the holding for any of the purposes following (that is to say), mining or taking minerals, or digging or searching for minerals; ... cutting or taking timber or turf, ... opening or making roads, fences, drains, and watercourses; passing and re-passing to and from the sea shore with or without horses and carriages for exercising any right of property or royal franchise belonging to the landlord, viewing or examining at reasonable times the state of the holding and all buildings or improvements thereon; hunting, shooting, fishing ...

(6) The tenant shall not on his holding, without the consent of his landlord, open any house for the sale of intoxicating liquors.

Nothing contained in this section shall prejudice or affect any ejectment for nonpayment of rent instituted by a landlord whether before or after the commencement of a statutory term, in respect of rent accrued due for a holding before the commencement of such term.

During the continuance of a statutory term in a tenancy, same as hereinafter provided, the court may, on the application of the landlord, and upon being satisfied that he is desirous of resuming the holding or part thereof for some reasonable and sufficient purpose authorize the resumption thereof by the landlord upon such conditions as the court may think fit, ...

Provided that the rent of any holding subject to statutory conditions may be increased in respect of capital laid out by the landlord under agreement with the tenant to such an amount as may be agreed upon between landlord and tenant.

6.   ...The compensation payable ... in the case of a tenant disturbed in his holding by the act of a landlord after the passing of this act shall be as follows, in the case of holdings where the rent is thirty pounds or under, a sum not exceeding seven years rent; where the rent is above thirty pounds and not exceeding fifty pounds, a sum not exceeding five years rent; where the rent is above fifty pounds and not exceeding one hundred pounds, a sum not exceeding four years rent; where the rent is above one hundred pounds and not exceeding three hundred pounds, a sum not exceeding three years rent; where the rent is above three hundred pounds and not exceeding five hundred pounds, a sum not exceeding two years rent; where the rent is above five hundred pounds, a sum not exceeding one year's rent.

8.   (1) The tenant of any present tenancy to which this act applies, or such tenant and the landlord jointly, or the landlord, ... may from time to time during the continuance of such tenancy apply to the court to fix the fair rent to be paid by such tenant to the landlord for the holding, ...

        (3) Where the judicial rent (the rent fixed by the court) of any present tenancy has been fixed ... then, until the expiration of a term of fifteen years from the rent day next succeeding the day on which the determination of the court has been given (in this act referred to as a statutory term), such present tenancy shall (if it so long continue to subsist) be deemed to be a tenancy subject to statutory conditions...

        (6) Subject to rules made under this act, the landlord and tenant of any present tenancy to which this act applies, may .. by writing under their hands, agree and declare what is then the fair rent of the holding; and such agreement and declaration on being filed in court in the prescribed manner, shall have the same effect and consequences in all respects as if the rent so agreed on were a judicial rent ...

10.   The landlord and tenant of any ordinary tenancy and the landlord and proposed tenant of any holding to which this act applies which is not subject to a subsisting tenancy, may agree, the one to grant and the other to accept a lease for a term of thirty-one years or upwards (in this act referred to as a judicial lease), on such conditions and containing such provisions as the parties to such lease may mutually agree upon, and such lease ... shall be substituted for the former tenancy, if any, in the holding ...

13.   (1) Where proceedings are or have been taken by the landlord to compel a tenant to quit his holding, the tenant may sell his tenancy at any time before but not after the expiration of six months from the execution of a writ or decree for possession in an ejectment for non-payment of rent, and at any time before but not after the execution of such writ or decree in any ejectment other than for nonpayment of rent; and any such tenancy so sold shall be and be deemed to be a subsisting tenancy notwithstanding such proceedings, without prejudice to the landlord's rights, in the event of the said tenancy not being redeemed within said period of six months; and, if any judgment or decree in ejectment has been obtained before the passing of this act, such tenant may within the same periods respectively apply to the court to fix the judicial rent of the holding, but subject to the provisions

herein contained such application shall not invalidate or prejudice any such judgment or decree, which shall remain in full force and effect.

(3). Where any proceedings for compelling the tenant of a present tenancy to quit his holding shall have been taken before or after an application to fix a judicial rent and shall be pending before such application is disposed of, the court before which such proceedings are pending shall have power ... to postpone or suspend such proceedings until the termination of the proceedings on the application for such judicial rent;....

(6) A tenant compelled to quit his holding during the continuance of a statutory term in his tenancy, in consequence of the breach by the tenant of any statutory condition, shall not be entitled to compensation for disturbance.

22.   A tenant whose holding or the aggregate of whose holdings is valued under the act relating to the valuation of rateable property in Ireland at an annual value of not less than one hundred and fifty pounds, shall be entitled by writing under his hand to contract himself out of any of the provisions of this act or of the <u>Landlord and Tenant (Ireland) Act, 1870</u>.

24.   (1) The land commission, out of moneys in their hands, may, if s satisfied with the security, advance sums to tenants for the purpose of enabling them to purchase their holdings, that is to say, --

(a) Where a sale of a holding is about to be made by a landlord to a tenant in consideration of the payment of a principal sum, the land commission may advance to the tenant for the purposes of such purchase, any sum not exceeding three fourths of the said principal sum.

(b) Where a sale of a holding is about to be made by a landlord to a tenant in consideration of the tenant paying a fine and engaging to pay to the landlord a fee farm rent, the land commission may advance to the tenant for the purposes of such purchase, any sum not exceeding one half of the fine payable to the landlord.

26.   (1) Any estate may be purchased by the land commission for the purpose of reselling to the tenants of the lands comprised in such estate their respective holdings, if the land commission are satisfied ... that a competent number of the tenants are able and willing to purchase their holdings from the land commission.

(2) The sale by the land commission of a holding to the tenant thereof may be made either in consideration of a principal sum being paid as the whole price ... or in consideration of a fine and of a fee farm rent, with this qualification, that the amount of the fee farm rent shall not exceed sevety-five percent of the rent which in the opinion of the land commission would be a fair rent for the holding.

(3) For the purposes of this section a competent number of tenants means a body of tenants who are not less in number than three fourths of the whole number of tenants on the estate, and who pay rent not less than two thirds of the whole rent of the estate, ...

28.   (1) Any advance made by the land commission for the purpose of supplying money for the purchase of a holding from a landlord or of a hold-

ing or parcel from the land commission, shall be repaid by an annuity in favour of the land commission for thirty-five years of five pounds for every hundred pounds os such advance, and so in proportion for any less sum.

37.   (1) The expression "the court" as used in this act shall mean the civil bill court of the county where the matter requiring the cognizance of the court arises.

(3) Any proceedings which might be instituted before the civil bill court may, at the election of the person taking such proceedings, be instituted before the land commission, ...

40.   Any matter capable of being determined by the court under this act, may, if the parties so agree, be decided by arbitration, ... and where the amount of rent is decided by arbitration, such rent shall for the purposes of this act be deemed to be the judicial rent.

41.   A land commission shall be constituted under this act consisting of a judicial commissioner and two other commissioners.

43.   The lord lieutenant may from time to time, with the consent of the treasury as to number, appoint and by order in council remove assistant commissioners, ...

44.   Any power or act by this act vested in or authorized to be done by the land commission, except the power of hearing appeals, may be exercised or done by any one member of the land commission or by any sub-commission, ...

PARNELL AND HOME RULE: SPEECH AT WICKLOW, 1885

Source: The Freeman's Journal, October 6, 1885.

When I last spoke in public in Ireland I expressed my conviction that
in the new parliament we should be able to form our platform of a single
plank, and that plank the plank of legislative independence (cheers), and
that we should carry that plank to a successful issue in the same way as
during the last parliament we have carried other subordinate planks, such
as the extension of the franchise and so forth (cheers). My declaration
has been received by the English press and by some, although not by all,
the English leaders with a storm of disapproval, and they have told us that
the yielding of an independent parliament to Ireland is a matter of impossibility. But nothing that has been said in this interval has in the slightest d-
degree diminished my confidence in the near success of our efforts (loud
cheers). On the contrary, very much that has been said by our enemies
in reference to this cliam of ours has very much increased my confidence
(cheers). They practically admit that things cannot be allowed to go on as
they are; that it is impossible to keep an unwilling people and unwilling representatives in forced legislative connexion with the other two kingdoms
(hear, hear). They admit that there must be some change; but the two conditions that they put forward in regard to this change, and as a condition of
this change, are -- firstly, that the separation of Ireland from England
shall not be a consequence of the grant of legislative independence to Ireland; and, in the second place, they claim that we shall not be allowed to
protect our manufactures at the cost of those of England. ... To take the
last point first, and to deal with the question of the protection of Irish manufactures, I have claimed for Ireland a parliament that shall have power to
protect these Irish manufactures (cheers), if it be the will of the parliament
and of the Irish people that they should be protected (cheers). But it is not
for me to say beforehand what the action of such a freely elected Irish assembly would be. I may have my own opinion as to the best course for
that assembly to take, but I have claimed that no parliamentary assembly
will work satisfactorily which has not free power over Irish affairs (applause); which has not free power to raise a revenue for the purpose of
government in Ireland as shall seem fit and best to that assembly (applause).
I am of the opinion -- an opinion that I had expressed before now -- that it
would be wise to protect certain Irish industries at all events for a time
(hear, hear); that it is impossible for us to make up for the loss of the start
in the manufacturing race which we have experienced owing to adverse legislation in times past against Irish industries by England, unless we do
protect these industries, not many in number, which are capable of thriv-
ing in Ireland (applause). I am not of the opinion that it would be necessary
for us to protect these industries very long, possibly protection continued

for two or three years would give us that start which we have lost, owing
to the nefarious legislative action of England in times past (hear, hear).
I think also that Ireland could never be a manufacturing nation of such im-
portance as to compete to any great extent with England. I believe there
are several industries which would thrive, and could be made to thrive, in
Ireland. But I think that, as regards many other branches of manufacture,
of which we have now to seek our supply from the English markets, we
should still have to go to their markets for supply on account of natural reasons which I have not time to enter into at the present moment. But I
claim this for Ireland, that if the Irish parliament of the future considers
that there are certain industries in Ireland which could be benefited by protection, which could be nursed by protection, and which could be placed in
such a position as to enable them to compete with similar industries in
other countries by a course of protection extending over a few years, the
parliament ought to have power to carry out that policy (cheers). It is not
for me to predict the extent to which that power should be used; but I tell
English radicals and English liberals that it is useless for them to talk of
their desire to do justice to Ireland when, from motives of selfishness,
they refused to repair that injustice by giving us the power which we think
would be sufficient to enable us to build up these comparatively few industries which Ireland is adapted by her circumstances to excel in (applause).
I will proceed a little further, and I will deal with the claim that has been
put forward, that some guarantee should be given that the granting of legislative powers to Ireland should not lead to the separation of Ireland from
England. This claim is one which at first sight may seem a fair one. It
may appear preposterous, and it undoubtedly would be preposterous, to
ask England to concede to us an engine which we announced our intention of
using to bring about either separation of the two countries, or which we accepted silently with the intenation of so using it; but there is a great differ-
ence between having such an intention, and giving counter guarantees
against such an intention. It is not possible for human intelligence to fore-
cast the future in these matters; but we can point to this -- we can point to
the fact that under 85 years of parliamentary connexion with England, Ireland has become intensely disloyal and intensely disaffected (applause); the
notwithstanding the whig policy of so-called conciliation, alternative conciliation and coercion, and ameliorative measures, that disaffection has broad-
ened, deepened and intensified from day to day (cheers). Am I not, then,
entitled to assume that one of the roots of this disaffection and feeling of di
disloyalty is the assumption by England of the management of our affairs
(cheers). It is admitted that the present system can't go on, and what are
you going to put in its place? (Cries of 'Home Rule'.) My advice to English
statesmen considering this question would be this -- trust the Irish people
altogether or trust them not at all (cheers). Give with a full and open hand
-- give our people the power to legislate upon all their domestic concerns,
and you may depend upon one thing, that the desire for separation, the
means of winning separation at least, will not be increased or intensified

(cheers). Whatever chance the English rules may have of drawing to themselves the affection of the Irish people lies in destroying the abominable system of legislative union between the two countries by conceding fully and freely to Ireland the right to manage her own affairs. It is impossible for us to give guarantees, but we can point to the past; we can show that the record of English rule is a constant series of steps from bad to worse (cheers), that the condition of English power is more insecure and more unstable at the present moment than it has ever been (applause). We can point to the example of other countries; of Austria and of Hungary -- to the fact that Hungary having been conceded self-government became one of the strongest facts in the Austrian empire. We can show the powers that have been freely conceded to the colonies -- to the great colonies -- including this very power to protect their own industries against and at the expense of those of England. We can show that disaffection has disappeared in all the greater English colonies, that while the Irishman who goes to the United States of America carries with him a burning hatred of English rule (cheers); that while that burning hatred constantly lives in his heart, never leaves him, and is bequeathed to his children, the Irishman coming from the same village, and from the same parish, and from the same townland, equally maltreated, cast out on the road by the relentless landlord, who goes to one of the colonies of Canada or one of the colonies of Australia, and finds there another and a different system of English rule to that which he has been accustomed to at home, because to a great extent a loyal citizen and a strength and a prop to the community amongst whom his lot has been cast; that he forgets the little memories of his experience of England at home, and that he no longer continues to look upon the name of England as a symbol of oppression, and the badge of the misfortunes of his country (cheers). I say that it is possible, and that it is the duty of English statesmen at the present day to inquire and examine into these facts for themselves with their eyes open; and to cease the impossible task, which they admit to be impossible, of going forward in the continued misgovernment of Ireland and persisting in the government of our people by a people outside herself who know not her real wants (cheers); and if these lessons be learned, I am convinced that the English statesman who is great enough, and who is powerful enough to carry out these teachings, to enforce them on the acceptance of his countrymen, to give to Ireland full legislative liberty, full power to manage her own domestic concerns, will be regarded in the future by his countrymen as one who had removed the greatest peril to the English empire (hear, hear) -- a peril, I firmly believe, which if not removed will find some day, perhaps not in our time -- some year, perhaps not for many years to come, but will certainly find sooner or later, and it may be sooner than later, an opportunity of revenging itself -- (loud cheers) -- to the destruction of the British empire for the misfortunes, the oppressions, and the misgovernment of our country (loud cheers).

WILLIAM EWART GLADSTONE ON HOME RULE,
HOUSE OF COMMONS, APRIL 8, 1886

Source: <u>Parliamentary Debates,</u> Series 3; vol CCCIV, cols. 1036-85
(London: Hansard, 1886)

I could have wished, Mr. Speaker, on several grounds, that it had
been possible for me on this single occasion to open to the house the whole
of the policy and intentions of the government with respect to Ireland. The
two questions of land and of Irish government are, in our view, closely
and inseparably connected, for they are the two channels through which we
hope to find access, and effectual access, to that questions which is the
most vital of all -- namely the question of social order in Ireland. As I
have said, those two questions are in our view - whatever they may be in
that of anyone else -- they are in our view, for reasons which I cannot
now explain, inseparable the one from the other. But it is impossible for
me to attempt such a task....

Since the last half-century dawned we have been steadily engaged in
extending, as well as in consolidating, free institutions. I divide the period since the act of union with Ireland into two -- the first from 1800 to
1832, the epoch of what is still justly called the great reform act; and secondly, from 1833 to 1885. I do not know whether it has been as widely
observed as I think it deserves to be that, in the first of those periods --
32 years -- there wer no less than 11 years -- it may seem not much to
say, but wait for what is coming -- there were no less than 11 of those 32
years in which our statute book was free throughout the whole year from re
repressive legislation of an exceptional kind against Ireland. But in the 53
years since we advanced far in the career of liberal principles and actions
-- in those 53 years, from 1833-1885 -- there were but two years which
were entirely free from the action of this special legislation for Ireland.
Is not that of itself almost enough to prove we have arrived at the point
where it is necessary that we should take a careful and searching survey
of our position? ...

Well, Sir, what are the results that have been produced? This result above all -- and now I come to what I consider to be the basis of the
whole mischief -- that rightly or wrongly, yet in point of fact, law is discredited in Ireland, and discredited in Ireland upon this ground especially
-- that it comes to the people of that country with a foreign aspect, and in
a foreign garb. These coercion bills of ours, of course -- for it has become a matter of course -- I am speaking of the facts and not of the merits
-- these coercion bills are stiffly resisted by the members who represent
Ireland in parliament. The English mind, by cases of this kind and by the
tone of the press towards them, is estranged from the Irish people and the
Irish mind is estranged from the people of England and Scotland. I will
not speak of other circumstances attending the present state of Ireland,

but I do think that I am not assuming too much when I say that I have shown
enough in this comparatively brief review -- and I wish it could have been
briefer still -- to prove that, if coercion is to be the basis for legislation,
we must no longer be seeking, as we are always laudably seeking, to whit-
tle it down almost to nothing at the very first moment we begin, but we
must, like men, adopt it, hold by it, sternly enforce it, till its end has
been completely attained -- with what results to peace, good will and freedom I do not now stop to inquire. Our ineffectual and spurious coercion is
morally worn out. . . .

        Now, I enter upon another proposition to which I hardly expect broad
exception can be taken. I will not assume, I will not beg, the question,
whether the people of England and Scotland will ever administer that sort
of effectual coercion which I have placed in contrast with our timid and hes-
itating repressive measures; but this I will say, that the people of England
and Scotland will never resort to that alternative until they have tried every
other. Have they tried every other? Well, some we have tried, to which
I will refer. I have been concerned with some of them myself. But we have
not yet tried every alternative, because there is one -- not unknown to human experience -- on the contrary, widely known to various countries in the
world, where this dark and difficult problem has been solved by the comparatively natural and simple, though not always easy, expeidient of stripping
law of its foreign garm, and investing it with a domestic character. I am
not saying that this will succeed; I by no means beg the question at this moment; but this I will say, that Ireland, as far as I know, and speaking of
the great majority of the people of Ireland, believes it will succeed and
that experience elsewhere supports that conclusion. The case of Ireland,
though she is represented here not less fully than England or Scotland, is
not the same as that of England or Scotland. England, by her own strength,
and by her vast majority in this house, makes her own laws just as indepen-
dently as if she were not combined with two other countries. Scotland --
a small country, smaller than Ireland, but a country endowed with a spirit
so masculine that never in the long course of history, excepting for two
brief periods, each of a few years, was the superior strength of England
such as to enable her to put down the national freedom beyond the border
-- Scotland, wisely recognized by England, has been allowed and encouraged in this house to make her own laws as freely and as effectually as if
she had a representation six times as strong. The consequence is that the
mainspring of law in England is felt by the people to be English, the mainspring of law in Scotland is felt by the people to be Scotch; but the mainspring of law in Ireland is not felt by the people to be Irish, and I am bound
to say -- truth extorts from me the avowal -- that it cannot be felt to be
Irish in the same sense as it is English and Scotch. The net results of this
statement which I have laid before the house, because it was necessary as
the groundwork of my argument, are these -- in the first palce, I admit it
to be little less than a mockery to hold that the state of law and of facts con-
jointly, which I have endeavoured to describe, conduces to the real unity

of this great, noble, and world-wide empire. In the second place, something must be done, something is imperatively demanded from us to restore
to Ireland the first conditions of civil life -- the free course of law, the
liberty of every individual in the exercise of every legal right, the confidence of the people in the law, apart from which no country can be called,
in the full sense of the word, a civilized country, nor can there be given
to that country the blessings which it is the object of civilized society to
attain. Well, this is my introduction to the task I have to perform, and
now I ask attention to the problem we have before us.

It is a problem not unknown in the history of the world; it is really
this -- there can be no secret about it as far as we are concerned -- how to
reconcile imperial unity with diversity of legislation. Mr. Grattan not only
held these purposes to be reconcilable, but he did not scruple to go the
length of saying this -- "I demand the continued severance of the parliaments with a view to the continued and everlasting unity of the empire."
Was that a flight of rhetoric, and audacious paradox? No; it was the statement of a problem which other countries have solved, and under circumstances much more difficult than ours. We ourselves may be said to have
solved it, for I do not think that anyone will question the fact that, out of
the six last centuries, for five centuries at least Ireland has had a parliament separate from ours. That is a fact undeniable. Did that separation
of parliament destroy the unity of the British empire? Did it destroy it in
the 18th century? Do not suppose that I mean that harmony always prevailed between Ireland and England. We know very well there were causes
quite sufficient to account for a recurrence of discord. But I take the 18th
century alone. Can I be told that there was no unity of empire in the 18th
Century? Why, Sir, it was the century which saw our navy come it its supremacy. It was the century which witnessed the foundation of that great,
gigantic manufacturing industry which now overshadows the whole world.
It was, in a pre-eminent sense, the century of empire, and it was in a
sense, but too conspicuous, the century of wars. Those wars were carried on, that empire was maintained and enormously enlarged, that trade was
established, that navy was brought to supremacy when England and Ireland
had separate parliaments. Am I to be told that there was no unity of empire in that state of things? Well, Sir, what has happened elsewhere? Have
any other countries had to look this problem in the face? The last half-century -- the last 60 or 70 years since the great war -- has been particularly
rich in its experience of this subject and in the lessons which it has afford-
ed to us. There are many cases to which I might refer to show how practicable it is, or how practicable it has been found by others whom we are not
accustomed to look upon as our political superiors -- how practicable it
has been found by others to bring into existence what is termed local autonomy, and yet not to sacrifice, but to confirm imperial unity....

What is the essence of the union? That is the question. It is impossible to determine what is and what is not the repeal of the union, until you
settle what is the essence of the union. Well, I define the essence of the

union to be this -- that before the act of union there were two independent, separate, co-ordinate parliaments; after the act of union there was but one. A supreme statutory authority of the imperial parliament over Great Britain, Scotland, and Ireland as one United Kingdom was established by the act of union. That it is not intended, in the slightest degree to impair ...

I will deviate from my path for a moment to say a word upon the state of opinion in that wealthy, intelligent, and energetic portion of the Irish community which, as I have said, predominates in a certain portion of Ulster. Our duty is to adhere to sound general principles, and to give the utmost consideration we can to the opinions of that energetic minority. The first thing of all, I should say, is that if, upon any occasions, by any individual or section, violent measures have been threatened in certain emergencies, I think the best compliment I can pay to those who have threatened us is to take no notice whatever of the threats, but to treat them as momentary ebullitions, which will pass away with the fears from which they spring, and at the same time to adopt on our part every reasonable measure for disarming those fears. I cannot conceal the conviction that the voice of Ireland, as a whole, is at this moment clearly and constitutionally spoken. I cannot say it is otherwise when five-sixths of its lawfully-chosen representatives are of one mind in this matter. There is a counter voice; and I wish to know what is the claim of those by whom that counter voice is spoken, and how much is the scope and allowance we can give them. Certainly, sir, I cannot allow it to be said that a protestant minority in Ulster, orelsewhere, is to rule the question at large for Ireland. I am aware of no constitutional doctrine tolerable on which such a conclusion could be adopted or justified. But I think that the protestant minority should have its wishes considered to the utmost practicalbe extent in any form which they may assume.

Various schemes, short of refusing the demand of Ireland at large, have been proposed on behalf of Ulster. One scheme is, that Ulster itself, or, perhaps with more appearance of reason, a portion of Ulster, should be excluded from the operation of the bill we are about to introduce. Another scheme is, that certain rights with regard to certain subjects -- such, for example, as education and some other subjects -- should be reserved and should be placed, to a certain extent, under the control of provincial councils. These, I think, are the suggestions which reached me in different shapes; there may be others, But what I wish to say of them is this -- there is no one of them which has appeared to us to be so completely justified, either upon its merits or by the weight of opinion supporting and recommending it, as to warrant our including it in the bill and proposing it to parliament upon our responsibility. What we think is that such suggestions deserve careful and unprejudiced consideration. It may be that free discussion, which I have no doubt will largely take place after a bill such as we propose shall have been laid on the table of the house, may give to one of these proposals, or to some other proposals, a practical form, and that some such plan may be found to be recommended by a general or predominating approval. If it should be so, it will, at our hands, have the most favourable consideration, with every disposition to do what equity may appear to recommend....

In 1782 there were difficulties that we have not now before us. At any time it might have been very fairly said that no one could tell how a separate legislature would work unless it had under its control what is termed a responsible government. We have no such difficulty and no such excuse now. The problem of responsible government has been solved for us in our colonies. It works very well there; and in, perhaps, a dozen cases in different quarters of the globe it works to our perfect satisfaction. It may be interesting to the house if I recount the fact that that responsible government in the colonies was, I think, first established by one of our most distinguished statesmen, Earl Russell, when he held the office of colonial secretary in the government of Lord Melbourne. But it was a complete departure from established tradition; and, if I remember right, not more than two or three years before that generous and wise experiment was tried, Lord Russell had himself written a most able despatch to show that it could not be done; that with responsible government in the colonies you would have two centres of gravity and two sources of motion in the empire; while a united empire absolutely required that there should be but one, and that consequently the proposition could not be entertained....

There is only one subject more on which I feel it still necessary to detain the house. It is commonly said in England and Scotland -- and in the main it is, I think, truly said -- that we have for a great number of years been struggling to pass good laws for Ireland. We have sacrificed our time, we have neglected our own business, we have advanced our money -- which I do not think at all a great favour conferred on her -- and all this in the endeavour to give Ireland good laws. That is quite true in regard to the general course of legislation since 1829. But many of those laws have been passed under influences which can hardly be described otherwise than as influences of fear. Some of our laws have been passed in a spirit of grudging and of jealousy....

But, sir, I do not deny the general good intentions of parliament on a variety of great and conspicuous occasions, and its desire to pass good laws for Ireland. But let me say that, in order to work out the purposes of government, there is something more in this world occasionally required than even the passing of good laws. It is sometimes requisite not only that good laws should be passed, but also that they should be passed by the proper persons. The passing of many good laws is not enough in cases where the strong permanent instincts of the people, their distinctive marks of character, the situation and history of the country require not only that these laws should be good, but that they should proceed from a congenial and native source, and besides being good laws should be their own laws.

ARTHUR GRIFFITH'S SPEECH AT THE FIRST ANNUAL
NATIONAL COUNCIL CONVENTION OF SINN FEIN,
NOVEMBER 28, 1905

Source: The United Irishman, December 9, 1905

   ...I am in economics largely a follower of the man who thwarted
England's dream of the commercial conquest of the world, and who made
the mighty confederation before which England has fallen commercially
and is falling politically -- Germany. His name is a famous one in the outside world, his works are the text books of economic science in other countries -- in Ireland his name is unknown and his works unheard of -- I refer to Frederick List, the real founder of the German Zollverein -- ...
   Brushing aside the fallacies of Adam Smith and his tribe, List points
out that between the individual and humanity stands, and must continue to
stand, a great fact -- the nation. The nation, with its special language and
literature, with it peculiar origin and history, with its special manners
and customs, laws and institutions, with the claims of all these for existence, independence, perfection, and continuance for the future, with its
separate territory, a society which, united by a thousand ties of minds and
interests, combines itself into one independent whole, which recognizes
the law of right for and within itself, and in its united character is still opposed to other societies of a similar kind in their national liberty, and consequently can, only under the existing conditions of the world, maintain
self-existence and independence by its own power and resources. As the
individual chiefly obtains by means of the nation and in the nation, mental
culture, power of production, security and prosperity, so is the civilization
of the human race only conceivable and possible by means of the civilization and development of individual nations. But as there are amongst men
infinite differences in condition and circumstances, so there are in nations
-- some are strong, some are weak, some are highly civilized, some are
held civilized, but in all exists as in the unit the impulse of self-preserva-
tion and the desire for improvement. It is the task of national politics to
ensure existence and continuance to the nation to make the weak strong, the
half civilized more civilized. It is the task of the national economics to
accomplish the economical development of the nation and fit it for admission into the universal society of the future....
   We in Ireland have been taught by our British lords lieutenant, our
British educational boards, and our Barrington lectures, that our destiny
is to be the fruitful mother of flocks and herds -- that it is not necessary
for us to pay attention to our manufacturing arm, since our agricultural
arm is all sufficient. The fallacy is apparent to the man who thinks -- but
it is a fallcy which has passed for truth in Ireland. With List I reply: a nation cannot promote and further its civilization, its prosperity, and its so-

cial progress equally as well by exchanging agricultural products for manufactured goods as by establishing a manufacturing power of its own. A
merely agricultural nation can never develop to any extent a home or foreign commerce, with inland means of transport, and its foreign navigation,
increase it population in due proportion to their well-being or make notable
progress in its moral, intellectual, social and political development; it
will never acquire important political power or be placed in a position to
influence less advanced nations and to form colonies of its own. A mere
agricultural state is infinitely less powerful than an agricultural-manufacturing state. The former is always economically and politically dependent
on those foreign nations who take from it agriculture in exchange for manufactured goods. . . . An agricultural nation is a man with one arm who makes
use of an arm belonging to another person, but cannot, of course, be sure
of having it always available. An agricultural-manufacturing nation is a
man who has both arms of his own at his own disposal. . . . We must offer
our producers protection where protection is necessary; and let it be clearly understood what protection is. Protection does not mean the exclusion
of foreign competition; it means the enabling of the native manufacturer to
meet foreign competition on an equal footing. It does not mean that we shall
pay a higher profit to any Irish manufacturer, but that we shall not stand
by and see him crushed by mere weight of foreign capital. If an Irish manufacturer cannot produce an article as cheaply as an English or other for-
eigner, solely because his foreign competitor has had larger resources at
his disposal, then it is the first duty of the Irish nation to accord protection
to the Irish manufacturer. If, on the other hand, an Irish manufacturer can
produce as cheaply, but charges an enhanced price, such a man deserves
no support -- he is in plain words a swindler. It is the duty of our public
bodies in whose hands the expenditure of £4,000,000 annually is placed to
pay where necessary an enhanced price for Irish manufactured articles,
when the manufacturers show them they cannot produce them at the lesser
price -- this is protection .... With the development of her manufacturing
arm will proceed the rise of a national middle class in Ireland and a trained national democracy and -- I here again quote List against the charlatans
who profess to see in a nation's language and tradition things of no economic
value -- "in every nation will the authority of national language and national literature, the civilizing arts and the perfection of municipal institutions
keep pace with the development of the manufacturing arm." How are we to
accord protection to and procure the development of our manufacturing arm?
First, by ourselves individually -- seconly, through our county, urban, and
district councils, and poor law guardans, thirdly, by taking over control of
those inefficient bodies known as harbour commissioners; fourthly, by
stimulating our manufacturers and our people to industrial enterprise; and
fifthly, by inviting to aid in our development, on commercial lines, Irish-
American capital. In the first case, every individual knows his duty,
whether he practises it or not -- it is, unless where fraud is attempted,
to pay if necessary an enhanced price for Irish goods, and to use whenever

possible none but Irish goods. As to our public elective bodies which annually control the expenditure of our local taxation, their duty is the same.
The duty of our harbour bodies is to arrange the incidence of purt dues so
that they shall fall most heavily on manufactured goods coming into the
country,, and to keep and publish a table of all goods imported and to whom
consigned. . . .

     We propose the formation of a Council of Three Hundred, composed
of members of the general council of county councils and representatives
of the urban councils, rural councils, poor law boards, and harbour boards
of the country to sit in Dublin and form a de facto Irish parliament. Associated and sitting and voting with this body, which might assemble in Dublin in the spring and in the autumn, could be the persons elected for Irish
constituencies, who decline to confer on the affairs of Ireland with foreigners in a foreign city. On its assembly in Dublin this national assembly
should appoint committees to especially consider and report to the general
assembly on all subjects appertaining to the country. On the reports of
these committees the council should deliberate and formulate workable
schemes, which, once formulated, it would be the duty of all county, councils, urban councils, poor law boards, and other bodies to give legal effect
to so far as their powers permit, and where their legal powers fall short,
to give it the moral force of law by inducing and instructing those whom they
represent to honour and obey the recommendations of the Council of Three
Hundred individually and collectively.

ULSTER'S SOLEMN LEAGUE AND COVENANT, 1912

Source: Belfast News-Letter, September 28, 1912.

Being convinced in our consciences that Home Rule would be disastrous to the material well-being of Ulster as well as of the whole of Ireland, subversive of our civil and religious freedom, destructive of our citizenship, and perilous to the unity of the empire, we, whose names are underwritten, men of Ulster, loyal subjects of His Gracious Majesty King George V, humbly relying on the God whom our fathers in days of stress and trial confidently trusted, do hereby pledge ourselves in solemn covenant throughout this our time of threatened calamity to stand by one another in defending for ourselves and our children our cherished position of equal citizenship in the United Kingdom, and in using all means which may be found necessary to defeat the present conspiracy to set up a Home Rule parliament in Ireland. And in the event of such a parliament being
forced upon us we further solemnly and mutually pledge ourselves to refuse to recognize its authority. In sure confidence that God will defend the right we hereto subscribe our names. And further, we individually declare that we have not already signed this covenant. God save the king.

SIR EDWARD CARSON, ON THE POSITION OF ULSTER,
HOUSE OF COMMONS, FEBRUARY 11, 1914

Source: <u>Parliamentary Debates</u>, Series 5, vol. LVIII, cols. 171-7
(London: H. M. Stationery Office, 1914)

... The speech from the throne talks of the fears of these men. Yes,
they have, I think, genuine fears for their civil and religious liberty under
the bill, but do not imagine that that is all that these men are fighting for.
They are fighting for a great principle, and a great ideal. They are fighting to stay under the government which they were invited to come under,
under which they have flourished, and under which they are content, and
to refuse to come under a government which they loath and detest. Men do
not make sacrifices or take up the attitude these men in Ulster have taken
up on a question of detail or paper safeguards. I am not going to argue it,
because they have thoroughly made up their minds, but I say this: If these
men are not morally justified when they are attempted to be driven out of
one government with which they are satisfied and put under another which
they loath, I do not see how resistance ever can be justified in history at
all. There was one point made by the prime minister yesterday, and re-
peated by Lord Morley in another place which I should like to deal with for
one moment, although it has been already referred to by my right hon.
friend last night. The prime minister said, it is "as the price of peace
that any suggestion we make will be put forward" (Official Report, 10 February 1914, col 82) and he elaborated that by saying that he did not mean the
mere abandonment of resistance, but that he meant that the bill, if these
changes were made, as I understand him, should as the price of changes
be accepted generally by opponents in Ireland, and in the unionist party, so
as to give, as he hoped, a good chance and send-off to the bill. If he means
that as the condition of the changes in the bill wer are to support the bill
or take any responsibility whatever for it, I tell him we never can do it.
Ulster looms very largely in this controversy, simply because Ulster has
a strong right arm, but there are unionists in the south and west who loath
the bill just as much as we Ulster people loath it, whose difficulties are
far greater, and who sould willingly fight, as Ulster would fight, if they had
the numbers. Nobody knows the difficulties of these men better than I do.
Why, it was only the other day some of them ventured to put forward as a
business proposition that this bill would be financial ruin to their businesses,
saying no more, and immediately they were boycotted, and resolutions
were passed, and they were told that they ought to understand as protestants
that they ought to be thankful and grateful for being allowed to live in peace
among the people who are there. Yes, we can never support the bill which
hands these people over to the tender mercies of those who have always been
their bitterest enemies. We must go on whatever happens, opposing the
bill to the end. That we are entitled to do; that we are bound to do. But I

want to speak explicitly about the exclusion of Ulster.... If the exclusion
of Ulster is not shut out, and if at the same time the prime minister says
he cannot admit anything contrary to the fundamental principles of the bill,
I think it follows that the exclusion of Ulster is not contrary to the fundamental principles of the bill. If that is so, are you really going on to these
grave difficulties in the future that the gracious speech from the throne
deals with, and not going to make your offer now, at once, with a view,
not to our adopting the bill, but to putting an end to resistance in Ulster.
Why do you hesitate? Surely something that is not fundamental to the principles of the bill is a thing that you may readily concede, rather than face
these grave difficulties which you yourselves admit to exist. I can only
say this to the prime minister: If the exclusion for that purpose is proposed, it will be my duty to go to Ulster at once and take counsel with the
people there; for I certainly do not mean that Ulster should be any pawn in
any political game. I say once more, that no responsible leader, unless
he were a lunatic, as the secretary of state says I am --

The Secretary of State for War (Colonel Seely): Mr. Speaker, if I
have ever said an unkind thing about the right non. gentleman, I unreservedly withdraw it; perhaps he will unreservedly withdraw the unkind things
which he may have said about me (An Hon. member: "They are always eat-
ing their words.")

Sir E. Carson: No responsible man, whether he was a leader or follower, could possibly go to the people, under any condition, and say, "We
are offered something," but say to them that, for political purposes, "You
ought to prepare to fight for it rather than accept it"; and I am not going to
do anything of the kind.

On the other hand I say this, that if your suggestions -- no matter
what paper safeguards you put, or no matter what other methods you may
attempt to surround these safeguards with for the purpose of raising what
I call "your reasonable atmosphere" -- if your suggestions try to compel
these people to come into a Dublin parliament, I tell you I shall, regardless
of personal consequences, go on with these people to the end with their policy of resistance. Believe me, whatever way you settle the Irish question,
there are only two ways to deal with Ulster. It is for statesmen to say
which is the best and right one. She is not a part of the community which
can be bought. She will not allow herself to be sold. You must therefore
either coerce her if you go on, in the long run, by showing that good government can come under the Home Rule bill, try and win her over to the
case of the rest of Ireland. You probably can coerce her -- though I doubt
it. If you do, what will be the disastrous consequences not only to Ulster,
but to this country and the empire? Will my fellow-countryman, the leader
of the Nationalist party, have gained anything? I will agree with him -- I
do not believe he wants to triumph any more than I do. But will he have
gained anything if he takes over these people and then applies for what he
used to call -- at all events his party used to call -- the enemies of the
people to come in and coerce them into obedience? No, sir, one false step

taken in relation to Ulster will, in my opinion, render for ever impossible
a solution of the Irish question. I say this to my nationalist fellow-coun-
trymen, and, indeed also to the government: you have never tried to win
over Ulster. You have never tried to understand her position. You have
never alleged, and can never allege, that this bill gives her one atom of
advantage. Nay, you cannot deny that it takes away many advantages that
she has as a constituent part of the United Kingdom. You cannot deny that
in the past she had produced the most loyal and law-abiding part of the citizens of Ireland. After all that, for these two years, every time we came
before you your only answer to us -- the majority of you, at all events --
was to insult us, and to make little of us. I say to the leader of the Nationalist party, if you want Ulster, go and take her, or go on and win her.
You have never wanted her affections; you have wanted her taxes.

THE EASTER REBELLION, 1916:
PROCLAMATION OF THE REPUBLIC

Source: The Times (London), April 26, 1916.

> The Provisional Goverment of the Irish republic to the
> people of Ireland

Irishmen and Irishwomen: In the name of God and of the dead generations from which she receives her old tradition of nationhood, Ireland,
through us, summons her children to her flag and strikes for her freedom.

Having organized and trained her manhood through her secret revolutionary organization, the Irish Republican Brotherhood, and through her open
open military organizations, the Irish Volunteers, and the Irish Citizen
Army, having patiently perfected her discipline, having resolutely waited
for the right moment to reveal itself, she now seizes that moment, and,
supported by her exiled children in Amerca and by gallant allies in Europe,
but relying in the first on her own strength, she strikes in full confidence
of victory.

We declare the right of the people of Ireland to the ownership of Ireland, and to the unfettered control of Irish destinies, to be sovereign and
indefeasible. The long usurpation of that right by a foreign people and government has not extinguished the right, nor can it ever be extinguished except by the destruction of the Irish people. In every generation the Irish
people have asserted their right to national freedom and sovereignty; six
times during the past three hundred years they have asserted it in arms.
Standing on that fundamental right and again asserting it in arms in the
face of the world, we hereby proclaim the Irish republic as a sovereign independent state, and we pledge our lives and the lives of our comrades-in-
arms to the cause of its freedom, of its welfare, and of its exaltation among
the nations.

The Irish republic is entitled to, and hereby claims, the allegiance
of every Irishman and Irishwoman. The republic guarantees religious and
civil liberty, equal rights and equal opportunities to all its citizens, and
declares its resolve to pursue the happiness and prosperity of the whole
nation and of all its party, cherishing all the children of the nation equally,
and oblivious of the differences carefully fostered by an alien government,
which have divided an minority from the majority in the past.

Until our arms have brought the opportune moment for the establishment of a permanent national government, representative of the whole people of Ireland, and elected by the suffrages of all her men and women, the
Provisional Government, hereby constituted, will administer the civil and
military affairs of the republic in trust for the people. We place the cause
of the Irish republic under the protection of the Most High God, whose blessing we invoke upon our arms, and we pray that no one who serves that

cause will dishonour it by cowardice, inhumanity, or rapine. In this supreme hour the Irish nation must, by its valour and discipline, and by the readiness of its children to sacrifice themselves for the common good, prove itself worthy of the august destiny to which it is called.

Signed on behalf of the provisional government,

Thomas J. Clarke, Sean MacDiarmada, Thomas MacDonagh, P. H. Pearse, Eamonn Ceannt, James Connolly, Joseph Plunkett.

MANIFESTO ISSUED BY SINN FEIN ON THE EVE OF
THE GENERAL ELECTION, 1918.

Source: Irish Times, December 5, 1918.

MANIFESTO TO THE IRISH PEOPLE

The coming General Election is fraught with vital possibilities for the future of our nation. Ireland is faced with the question whether this generation wills it that she is to march out into the full sunlight of freedom, or is to remain in the shadow of a base imperialism that has brought and ever will bring in its train naught but evil for our race.

Sinn Fein gives Ireland the opportunity of vindicating her honour and pursuing with renewed confidence the path of national salvation by rallying to the flag of the Irish Republic.

Sinn Fein aims at securing the establishment of that Republic.

1. By withdrawing the Irish Representation from the British Parliament and by denying the right and opposing the will of the British Government or any other foreign Government to legislate for Ireland.

2. By making use of any and every means available to render impotent the power of England to hold Ireland in subjection by military force or otherwise.

3. By the establishment of a constitutent assembly comprising persons chosen by Irish constituencies as the supreme national authority to speak and act in the name of the Irish people, and to develop Ireland's social, political and industrial life, for the welfare of the whole people of Ireland.

4. By appealing to the Peace Conference for the establishment of Ireland as an Independent Nation. At that conference the future of the nations of the world will be settled on the principle of government by consent of the governed. Ireland's claim to the application of that principle in her favour is not based on any accidental situation arising from the war. It is older than many if not all of the present belligerents. It is based on our unbroken tradition of nationhood, on a unity in a national name which has never been challenged on our possession of a distinctive national culture and social order, on the moral courage and dignity of our people in the face of alien aggression, on the fact that in nearly every generation, and five times within the past 120 years, our people have challenged in arms the right of England to rule this country. On these incontrovertible facts is based the claim that our people have beyond question established the right to be accorded all th power of a free nation.

Sinn Fein stands less for a political party than for the Nation; it represents the old tradition of nationhood handed on from dead generations; it stands by the Proclamation of the Provisional Government of Easter, 1916, reasserting the inalienable right of the Irish Nation to sovereign independence, reaffirming the determination of the Irish people to achieve it, and guaranteeing within the independent Nation equal rights and equal opportunities to all its citizens.

Believing that the time has arrived when Ireland's voice for the principle of untrammelled National self-determination should be heard above every interest of party or class, Sinn Fein will oppose at the Polls every individual candidate who does not accept this principle.

The policy of our opponents stands condemned on any test, whether of principle or expediency. The right of a nation to sovereign independence rests upon immutable natural law and cannot be made the subject of a compromise. Any attempt to barter away the sacred and inviolate rights of nationhood begins in dishonour and is bound to end in disaster. The enforced exodus of millions of our people, the decay of our industrial life, the ever-increasing financial plunder of our country, the whittling down of the demand for the 'Repeal of the Union' voiced by the first Irish Leader to plead in the Hall of the Conqueror to that of Home Rule on the Statute Book, and finally the contemplated mutilation of our country by partition, are some of the ghastly results of a policy that leads to national ruin.

Those who have endeavoured to harness the people of Ireland to England's war chariot, ignoring the fact that only a freely-elected Government in a free Ireland has power to decide for Ireland the question of peace and war, have forfeited the right to speak for the Irish people. The Green Flag turned red in the hands of the Leaders, but that shame is not to be laid at the doors of the Irish people unless they continue a policy of sending their representatives to an alien and hostile assembly, whose powerful influence has been sufficient to destroy the integrity and sap the independence of their representatives. Ireland must repudiate the men who, in a supreme crisis for the nation, attempted to sell her birthright for the vague promises of English ministers, and who showed their incompetence by failing to have even these promises fulfilled.

The present Irish members of the English Parliament constitute an obstacle to be removed from the path that leads to the Peace Conference. By declaring their will to accept the status of a province instead of boldly taking their stand upon the right of the nation they supply England with the only subterfuge at her disposal for obscuring the issue in the eyes of the world. By their persistent endeavours to induce the young manhood of Ireland to don the uniform of our seven-century old oppressor, and place their lives at the disposal of the military machine that holds our nation in bondage, they endeavour to barter away and even to use against itself the one great asset still left to our Nation after the havoc of centuries.

Sinn Féin goes to the polls handicapped by all the arts and contrivances that a powerful and unscrupulous enemy can use against us. Conscious of the power of Sinn Féin to secure the freedom of Ireland the British Government would destroy it. Sinn Féin, however, goes to the polls confident that the people of this ancient nation will be true to the old cause and will vote for the men who stand by the principles of Tone,

Emmet, Mitchel, Pearse and Connolly, the men who disdain to whine to the enemy for favours, the men who hold that Ireland must be as free as England or Holland, or Switzerland or France, and whose demand is that the only status befitting this ancient realm is the status of a free nation.

DECLARATION OF INDEPENDENCE
ADOPTED BY DAIL EIREANN, 1919

Source: Irish Times, January 22, 1919

Whereas the Irish people is by right a free people:

And whereas for seven hundred years the Irish people has never ceased to repudiate and has repeatedly protested in arms against foreign usurpation;

And whereas English rule in this country is, and always has been, based upon force and fraud and maintained by military occupation against the declared will of the people;

And whereas the Irish Republic was proclaimed in Dublin on Easter Monday, 1916, by the Irish Republican Army, acting on behalf of the Irish people;

And whereas the Irish people is resolved to secure and maintain its complete independence in order to promote the common weal, to re-establish justice, to provide for future defence, to ensure peace at home and good will with all nations, and to constitute a national policy based upon the people's will, with equal right and equal opportunity for every citizen;

And whereas at the threshold of a new era in history the Irish electorate has in the General Election of December, 1918, seized the first occasion to declare by an overwhelming majority its firm allegiance to the Irish Republic;

Now, therefore, we, the elected Representatives of the ancient Irish people in National Parliament assembled, do, in the name of the Irish Nation, ratify the establishment of the Irish Republic and pledge ourselves and our people to make this declaration effective by every means at our command;

We ordain that the elected Representatives of the Irish people alone have power to make laws binding on the people of Ireland, and that the Irish Parliament is the only Parliament to which that people will give its allegiance;

We solemnly declare foreign government in Ireland to be an invasion of our national right which we will never tolerate, and we demand the evacuation of our country by the English Garrison;

We claim for our national independence the recognition and support of every free nation in the world, and we proclaim that independence to be a condition precedent to international peace thereafter;

In the name of the Irish people we humbly commit our destiny to Almighty God Who gave our fathers the courage and determination to persevere through long centuries of a ruthless tyranny, and strong in the justice of the cause which they have handed down to us, we ask His Divine blessing on this the last stage of the struggle we have pledged ourselves to carry through to freedom.

THE BIRTH OF THE IRISH FREE STATE, 1921

Source: The Irish Times, December 10, 1921

Articles of Agreement for a Treaty between Great Britain
and Ireland, Dated the sixth day of December 1921

1.   Ireland shall have the same constitutional status in the community of nations known as the British Empire as the Dominion of Canada,
the Commonwealth of Australia, the Dominion of New Zealand, and the
Union of South Africa, with a parliament having powers to make laws for
the peace and good government of Ireland and an executive responsible to
that parliament, and shall be styled and known as the Irish Free State.

2.   Subject to the provisions hereinafter set out the position of
the Irish Free State in relation to the imperial parliament and government
and otherwise shall be that of the Dominion of Canada, and the law, practice and constitutional usage governing the relationship of the crown or the
representative of the crown and of the imperial parliament to the Dominion
of Canada shall govern their relationship to the Irish Free State.

3.   The representative of the crown in Ireland shall be appointed
in like manner as the governor-general of Canada, and in accordance with
the practice observed in the making of such appointments.

16. Neither the parliament of the Irish Free State nor the parliament of Northern Ireland shall make any law so as to either directly or indirectly to endow any religion or prohibit or restrict the free exercise
thereof or give any preference or impose any disability on account of religious belief or religious status or affect prejudicially the right of any child
to attend a school receiving public money without attending the religious
instruction at the school or make any discrimination as respects state aid
between schools under the management of different religious denominations
or divert from any religious denomination or any educational institution
any of its property except for public utility purposes and on payment of
compensation.

DAVID LLOYD GEORGE ON THE TREATY,
HOUSE OF COMMONS DECEMBER 14, 1921

Source: <u>Parliamentary Debates,</u> Series 5, vol CXLIX, cols. 25-49
(London: H. M. Stationery Office, 1922)

On the British side we have allegiance to the crown, partnership in
the empire, security of our shores, non-coercion of Ulster. These are
the provisions we have over and over again laid down, and they are here,
signed in this document.

On the Irish side there is one supreme condition -- that the Irish
people as a nation should be free in their own land to work out their own
national destinies in their own way. These two nations, I believe, will be
reconciled. Ireland, within her own boundaries, will be free to marshal
her own resources, direct her own forces -- material, moral and spiritual
-- and guide her own destinies. She has accepted allegiance to the crown,
partnership in the same empire, and subordinated her external relations
to the judgment of the same general council of the empire as we have. She
has agreed to freedom of choice for Ulster. The freedom of Ireland in-
creases the strength of the empire by ending the conflict which has been
carried on for centuries with varying success, but with unvarying discred-
it, for centuries. Incidents of that struggle have done more to impair the
honour of this country than any aspect of its world dominion throughout
the ages. It was not possible to interchange views with the truest friends
of Britain without feeling that there was something in reference to Ireland
to pass over. This brings new credit to the empire, and it brings new st
strength. It brings to our side a valiant comrade.

During the trying years of the war we set up for the first time in the
history of this empire a great imperial war cabinet. There were present
representatives of Canada, Australia, South Africa, New Zealand, and In-
dia, but there was one vacant chair, and we all were conscious of it. It
was the chair that ought to have been filled by Ireland. In so far as it was
occupied, it was occupied by the shadow of a fretful, resentful, angry people -- angry not merely for ancient wrongs, but angry because,while every
nation in the empire had its nationhoood honoured, the people who were a
nation when the oldest Dominion had not even been discovered had its nationhood ignored. The youngest Dominion marched into the war under its
own flag. As for the flag of Ireland, it was torn from the hands of men
who had volunteered to die for the cause which the British empire was
championing. The result was a rebellion, and, at the worst moment of the
war, we had to divert our minds to methods of dealing with the crisis in
Ireland. Henceforth that chair will be filled by a willing Ireland, radiant
because her long quarrel with Great Britain will have been settled by the
concession of liberty to her own people, and she can now take part in the
partnership of empire, not merely without loss of self-respect, but with an

accession of honour to herself and of glory to her own nationhood.

By this agreement we win to our side a nation of deep abiding and even passionate loyalties. What nation ever showed such loyalty to its faith under such conditions? Generations of persecution, proscription, beggary and disdain -- she faced them all. She showed loyalty to kings whom Britain had thrown over. Ireland stood by them, and shed her blood to maintain their inheritance -- that precious loyalty which she now avows to the throne, and to the partnership and common citizenship of empire. It would be taking too hopeful a view of the future to imagine that the last peril of the British empire has passed. There are still dangers lurking in the mists. Whence will they come? From what quarter? Who knows? But when they do come, I feel glad to know that Ireland will be there by our side, and the old motto that "England's danger is Ireland's opportunity" will have a new meaning. As in the case of the Dominions in 1914, our peril will be her danger, our fears will be her anxieties, our victories will be her joy.

DE VALERA AND THE REJECTION OF PARTITION, 1937-38

Sources: (1) Bunreacht na hEireann, Dublin, 1937
           (2) Evening Standard (London), October 17, 1938.

1. The Constitution of 1937

Article II: The national territory consists of the whole island of
                 Ireland, its islands and territorial seas ....
Article III: Pending the re-integration of the national territory,
                 and without prejudice to the right of the Parliament
                 and Government established by this Constitution to
                 exercise jurisdiction over the whole of that territory,
                 the laws of that Parliament shall have the like area and
                 extent of application as the laws of Saorstat Eireann
                 (the Irish Free State) and the like extra-territorial
                 effect.
Article IV: / The name of the state is_/ Eire, or in the English
                 language, Ireland.

2. Newspaper interview with Premier De Valera, 1938.

...Taking into account the prevailing sentiment of the present maj-
oirty of the Six Counties and bearing in mind also the sentiment of the minority there and the majority in the whole island, here is what I propose.
If I could have my own way, I would have immediately a single All-Ireland
Parliament elected on a system of proportional representation so as to be
fair to minorities -- this might entail a different form of executive. But
what I propose, in the existing situation, is not that. I would say to Belfast:
"Keep all your present powers. We only ask one thing of you. We think
the area you control is not the area which in justice you could claim, even
for a local parliament, but we make the concession if you guarantee fair
play for the minority and consent to the transfer to an All-Ireland Parliament of the powers now reserved to the Parliament at Westminster."

I want to make it as easy as possible for Northern Ireland to join us,
because it is my fixed belief that, once we are working together and prejudices eliminated, the North would speedily find it more economical and
satisfactory to surrender their local parliament altogether and come into
a single All-Ireland Parliament.

I.R.A. ULTIMATUM, 1939

Source: <u>The</u> <u>Times</u> (London), January 17, 1939.

On the twenty-third day of April in the year 1916 in the city of Dublin, seven men, who were representative in spirit and outlook and purpose of the Irish nation that had never yielded nor accepted the British conquest, set their humble and almost unknown names to the foregoing document that has passed into history, making the names of the seven signatories immortal.

Those signatures were sealed with the blood of the immortal seven, and of many others who followed them into one of the most gallant fights in the history of the world; and the Irish nation rose from shame to honour, from humiliation to pride, from slavery to freedom.

Three years later (on January 21, 1919), the Republic proclaimed in Easter week of 1916 was ratified and formally established by the elected representatives of all Ireland and a solemn declaration of independence sent out to the nations of the world.

To combat that declaration and to prevent the proclamation of the Republic of Ireland from becoming effective, the Armed Forced of the English enemy made war upon the people of this country. They were met by the Irish Republican Army, and challenged and resisted so stubbornly that after two years of warfare the English were forced to ask for a truce with a view to settlement by negotiation.

Unfortunately, because men were foolish enough to treat with an armed enemy within their gates, the English won the peace. Weakness and treachery caused a resumption of the war and the old English tactics of "Divide and Conquer" were exploited to the fullest extent. Partition was introduced, the country divided into two parts with two separate parliaments subject to and controlled by the British Government from London. The Armed Forces of England still occupy six of our counties in the North and reserve the right "in time of war or strained relations" to re-occupy the ports which they have just evacuated in the Southern part of Ireland. Ireland is still tied, as she has been for centuries past, to take part in England's wars. In the Six Counties, a large number of Republican soldiers are held prisoners by England. Further weakness on the part of some of our people, broken faith and make believe have postponed the enthronement of the living Republic, but the proclamation of Easter week and the Declaration of Independence stand and must stand forever. No man, no matter how far he has fallen away from his national faith, has dared to repudiate them. They constitute the rallying centre for the unbought manhood of Ireland in the fight that must be made to make them effective and to redeem the nation's self-respect that was abondoned by a section of our people in 1922.

The time has come to make that fight. There is no need to re-declare the Republic of Ireland, now or in the future. There is no need to re-affirm the Declaration of Irish Independence. But the hour has come for the supreme effort to make both effective. So in the name of the unconquered dead and of the faithful living, we pledge ourselves to that task.

We call upon England to withdraw her armed forces, her civilian officials and institutions, and representatives of all kinds from every part of Ireland, as an essential preliminary to arrangements for peace and friendship between the two countries; and we call upon the people of all Ireland, at home and in exile, to assist us in the effort we are about to make in God's name, to compel that evacuation and to enthrone the Republic of Ireland.

Signed on behalf of
The Republican Government and the Army
Council of Oglaigh na hEireann
(Irish Republican Army)

Stephen Hayes	Patrick Fleming
Peadar O'Flaherty	George Plunkett
Laurence Grogan	Sean Russell

A NEW STAGE IN ANGLO-IRISH RELATIONS, 1949

Source: <u>Public General Acts of the United Kingdom of Great Britain and
Ireland, 1949</u> (London, 1949), pp. 107 ff.

The Ireland Act (12 and 13 George VI, ch. 41).

1.   (1) It is hereby recognised and declared that the part of
                  Ireland heretofore known as Eire ceased, as from the
                  eighteenth day of April, nineteen hundred and forty-nine,
                  to be part of His Majesty's dominions.
             (2) It is hereby declared that Northern Ireland remains part
                  of His Majesty's dominions and of the United Kingdom
                  and it is hereby affirmed that in no event will Northern
                  Ireland or any part thereof cease to be part of His Maj-
                  esty's dominions and of the United Kingdom without the
                  consent of the Parliament of Northern Ireland.
             (3) The part of Ireland referred to in subsection (1) of this
                  section is hereafter in this Act referred to, and may in
                  any Act, enactment or instrument passed or made after
                  the passing of this Act be referred to, by the name at-
                  tributed thereto by the law thereof, that is to say, as
                  the Republic of Ireland.

2.   (1) It is hereby declared that, notwithstanding that the Re-
                  public of Ireland is not part of His Majesty's dominions,
                  the Republic of Ireland is not a foreign country for the
                  the purposes of any law in force in any part of the United
                  Kingdom or in any colongy, protectorate, or United
                  Kingdom trust territory. . . .

THE LAUNCHING OF A NEW I.R.A. CAMPAIGN, 1956

Source: The Irish Times, December 13, 1956

Statement Issued by the Army Council of the Irish Republican Army on December 12, 1956:

Resistance to British rule in occupied Ireland has now entered a decisive stage. Early today, Northern units of the Irish Republican Army attacked key British occupation installations.

Spearheaded by volunteers of the Irish Republican Army, our people in the Six Counties have carried the fight to the enemy. They are the direct victims of British Imperialism and they are also the backbone of the national revolutionary resurgence....

We call on Irish men in the British Armed Forces to stand by the motherland and refuse to bear arms against their own countrymen. We call on members of the R.U.C. and B Special Constabulary to cease being tools of British Imperialism and either stand on one side or join us in the fight against tyranny....

The foe will use his considerable resources to divide us by fanning the fires of bigotry and sectarianism -- twin enemies of the Irish Republicanism. Let us be on our guard, a free Ireland cannot tolerate the one or the other....

THE ULSTER QUESTION, 1969-72

Sources: (1) <u>Belfast Telegraph,</u> January 6, 1969.
          (2) <u>Belfast Telegraph,</u> May 10, 1969
          (3) <u>New York Times,</u> December 3, 1971
          (4) <u>New York Times,</u> June 13, 1972.

Statement by Premier O'Neill, January 5, 1969.

I want the people of Ulster to understand in plain terms the events
which have taken place since January 1st. The march to Londonderry
planned by the so-called People's Democracy was, from the outset, a fool-
hardy and irresponsible undertaking. At best, those who planned it were
careless of the effects it would have; at worst, they embraced with enthusiasm the prospect of adverse publicity causing further damage to the interests of Northern Ireland as a whole....
    ...Clearly Ulster has now had enough. We are all sick of marchers
and counter-marchers. Unless these warring minorities rapidly return to
their senses we will have to consider a further reinforcement of the regu-
lar police by greater use of the Special Constabulary for normal police
duties....
    I think we must also have an urgent look at the Public Order Act it-
self to see whether we ought to ask Parliament for further powers to control those elements which are seeking to hold the entire community to ran-
som.
    Enough is enough. We have heard sufficient for now about civil
rights; let us hear a little about civic responsibility. For it is a short step
from the throwing of paving stones to the laying of tombstones and I for one
can think of no cause in Ulster today which will be advanced by the death
of a single Ulsterman.   (1)

Newspaper Interview with Premier O'Neill, May 10, 1969

    ...It is frightfully hard to explain to Protestants that if you give Ro-
man Catholics a good job and a good house, they will live like Protestants,
because they will see neighbours with cars and television sets; they will
refuse to have eighteen children. But if a Roman Catholic is jobless, and
lives in the most ghastly hovel, he will rear eighteen children on National
Assistance. If you treat Roman Catholics with due consideration and kindness, they will live like Protestants in spite of the authoritative nature of
their Church ....   (2)

Harold Wilson, Leader of the Labour Party, in Commons, December
1971.

I believe that the situation has now gone so far that it is impossible to conceive of an effective long-term solution in which the agenda, at least, does not include consideration of, and which is not in some way directed to finding a means of achieving, the aspirations envisaged half a century ago of progress towards a united Ireland. (3)

William Whitelaw, Secretary of State for Northern Ireland, in Commons, June 12, 1972.

We don't intend to let part of the United Kingdom ... default from the rule of law at the behest of ruthless conspiracy. The disrespect for law rooted there tends to spread like a cancer to other places. I will take the sternest measures to stop the spread of that cancer elsewhere ... Our troops and our money are an eloquent testimony of our concern... (4)

WILLIAM WHITELAW ON THE SITUATION IN
NORTHERN IRELAND, 1972

Source: <u>New York Times,</u> June 22, 1972

I have set myself to make use of every possible approach -- diplomatic, blunt, direct, polite -- to persuade as many people as possible to join hands with me in making Northern Ireland a place where the man who wants to draw attention to his point of view doesn't have to depend on a loaded gun or a bomb for the purpose.

The istuation is not just about law and order. It is not simply a question of meeting a force of which we cannot approve with a greater force of which we can approve. If history is to pass judgment on the work we are trying to do now then please God let it not be, "They took the easy way out -- the way to short-term peace and long-term disaster."

Nor is the situation one where a single, straightforward move, whether by Protestants, Catholics, by us here in London or by statesmen anywhere in the world, will produce a solution as if by a wave of a magician's wand, in a flash.

Nevertheless this is not a situation in which there is no peace to be found. It is not beyond the wit of man to devise a solution. I know that those who want peace will triumph in the end. But the point of view is often put -- how can we hope to get anywhere with a problem that has defied the abilities of many of our politicians for centuries? The Irish will always fight among themselves, it is argued. Surely we should just wash our hands of the whole sorry mess? This I cannot possibly accept.

To begin with I doubt whether any of us would be in public life if we did not sincerely believe that it is in the power of man himself to right these wrongs which man himself has inflicted. That is the simple answer to those who say there is no peace to be found. But there is also a more specific answer. It is not a matter of votes won or lost, it is not an arguing point for academics. It is a brutal and brutalizing tragedy where grievous suffering and destruction is daily inflicted, where people are regularly maimed and disfigured for life, where the ultimate disaster of loss of life is an almost daily happening.

Fear is the constant companion of a great number of its people. Not just the physical fear of the bomb and the bullet but fear of the things their fathers feared. For a Protestant, fear that he will be handed over into a united Ireland against his will. For a Catholic, the fear that discrimination and political intimidation will bedevil his own life and that of his family. On both counts the British Government has made its position totally clear. Let me say it again. Without the consent of the majority of the people of Northern Ireland the United Kingdom Government will not countenance the absorption of the province into a united Ireland.

To the Catholics in Northern Ireland let me say that the security
forces will give their protection to all who are in need of it. There will
be no discrimination on the grounds of religion either in Norther Ireland,
or, indeed, anywhere else in the United Kingdom.

What then is to be done? If we were sure, in all likelihood I would
not be here tonight, for there would be no office of Secretary of State for
Northern Ireland, and the horrific events which have become such a de-
pressing feature of Ulster life would not be screaming at us from the head-
lines and the television sets. So we work and we think and we hope and we
pray.

It appalls me, as it must appall all people of good sense, to read of
behavior which puts men's jobs at risk. What good does it do any cause
to wage war on workpeople, to imperil their right to earn an honest livelihood, to prevent a man from trying to pay his way and do the best for his
family? I know now that I have a great reservoir of goodwill in Northern
Ireland on which I can draw in my efforts. And I know I have the united
people of Great Britain. What I am seeking to achieve is simple. I am
seeking the help of all in building a place with a real future, a place of
promise, a place where the voices that are loudest in the land are not the
voices of the wreckers and the chronically disgruntled.

And I am convinced that slowly -- and there are signs that it may be
already happening -- the two communities in Northern Ireland must learn
to come together and to live together. It will happen because it must happen. There are no martyrs in Northern Ireland. There are only victims.
The dying will have to stop. We are utterly determined that it should be
soon.

PREMIER LYNCH ON THE "ANGLO-IRISH PROBLEM," 1972

Source: John M. Lynch, "The Anglo-Irish Problem," <u>Foreign Affairs</u>,
Vol. 50, No. 4 (July 1972), 601-617

I consider that the only solution is an Ireland united by agreement,
in independence; an Ireland in a friendly relationship with Britain; an Ireland which will be a member with Britain of the enlarged European Communities. I hold this view because I believe that there is no other way to
dispose of the contentious and difficult legacy which history has left to our
two islands -- certainly no way which will not compound the problem for
our children. I shall try to be more specific. The points I set out below
are an attempt to outline some of the views which I believe any realistic
observer who studies the problem in any depth would come to.

Firstly, I consider that the decision by the British government to exercise its full responsibility for Northern Ireland direcly for one year from
March 1972 was a positive step because it meant a recognition that it was
not possible to work through the existing structures. But that step was pre-
sented only as a necessary preliminary to a solution and not as itself a
solution.

Secondly, I consider that any attempt to follow it up by integrating
Northern Ireland fully into the United Kingdom would be disastrous. A substantial minority in the North would permanently resist it with the support
of the great majority of the people of Ireland. Such an attempt would drive
a wedge between the majority populations of the two islands; and, as I have
explained, Northern Ireland cannot be dealt with without reference to the
Anglo-Irish relationship as a whole.

Thirdly, Britain should recognize that the more intransigent among
the Unionist minority in Ireland are not entitled to a permanent vote on harmony in Anglo-Irish relations; and recognizing this, should begin to work
toward a real settlement. Such a settlement should not impose unity by
force. But where the earlier settlement tended to encourage continuing division, this new settlement should offer positive and direct encouragement
to unity, accepting that the fears of a community of less than one million
should not stand permanently in the way of reconciliation between all the
peoples of both islands. Many of the Unionist community realize that Irish
unity is inevitable and are increasingly willing to consider the idea. They
should be offered positive and direct encouragement in that direction.

Fourthly, while I consider that the division of Ireland was misguided
from the outset, I recognize that obtaining unity is a difficult process.
There has to be a growth of trust and reconciliation on all sides. But I believe that Irish unity should be the aim, and a commitment should be made
by the British government to its achievement.

Fifthly, it should be clear that a united Ireland will not be an Ireland in which the present state in the "South" takes over the "North" and assimilates it into its existing structures. There should be negotiation, but it should be about a new Ireland.

Sixthly, the new Ireland to which I have referred should not involve any levelling down, on either side, of existing social or economic standards. There are dsicrepancies at present but they are not insurmountable and they are lessening. The real dividing line in Ireland so far as economic prosperity is concerned has always been an East-West and not a North-South one. At present the link with Britain provides substantial direct and indirect subsidies to Northern Ireland. In any settlement arrangements these subsidies would no doubt eventually have to be phased out; but this should be done over a period. Growing integration of the economies of all EEC member countries should help. Regional development policies of the EEC will also be helpful to each part of what is largely a single region -- as will the general increase in prosperity of all within the EEC. Beyond this, however, the aspect of a united Ireland which would be most conducive to long-term economic prosperity would be its ability to concentrate its energies on building a better life for its people -- instead of dissipating them, as at present, in division and recrimination.

What should be the constitution of this new Ireland? Obviously it must reflect the values and meet the legitimate interests of all sections of its population.

A constitution can take a number of forms. The British Constitution, for example, is not a single written document but a whole structure of conventions, laws, political institutions and established practices. What has often been referred to as the "Constitution of Northern Ireland" was simply an Act of the Westminster Parliament -- the Government of Ireland Act, 1920, as amended by subsequent enactments. The Irish Constitution on the other hand, like that of the United States, is a written one. It was adopted by referendum in 1937 and its provisions require any amendments to be adopted first by Parliament and then submitted to the people in referendum.

The 1937 Constitution as it stands is not suitable for a new Ireland. My own view is that it would be better to regard the new Ireland as an entirely new political entity which should work out and enact for itself its own constitution. I do not say this because of reluctance to consider the changes necessary for a new Ireland but on the contrary because I believe that a fresh start could be a better approach. This would not, however, exclude preparatory work being undertaken now.

Parnell said in 1886 that, "the best system of Government for a country / is_ / ... one which requires that that Government should be the resultant of all the forces within that country." I think something similar is true of the final working out of a constitution and system of government for a new Ireland. These are matters best worked out by the representatives of all those who are to live under the new structures. A philosopher or a constitutional lawyer may advise or draft a constitution; but he should not, I think, attempt to write the final version, at least not in a situation such

as ours in Ireland, where the building up of trust and the overcoming of
fears are so important.

The constitution of the new Ireland would have to be a written one with
firm and explicit guarantees for the rights and liberties of all who live under it. I would tend to favor the view that these guarantees should relate
to the individual citizens rather than to institutions as such. The constitution makers should perhaps take a "minimal" approach, i.e. not start
from broad philosophical assumptions but, instead, try to piece together
an agreement on what is necessary for government to function while ensur-
ing rights and liberties to the individual.

Though I have frequently referred in this article to the "Irish Question" it is no longer fashionable, as it once was, to speak of international
problems in terms of "Questions." Perhaps to do so implies that "answers"
exist, and there is a pessimistic tendency today to accept that some questions are unanswerable. But I do not believe that either Britain or Ireland
can accept this kind of thinking. In the Anglo-Irish relationship Northern
Ireland is a problem to which there is a solution; it is not an unanswerable
question.

The solution which I have outlined is that Ireland as a whole should
assert a new and more comprehensive identity.

What is it exactly that gives a people a sense of national identity?
What is it that determines how the first person plural -- the "we" -- shall
be used when a nation speaks of its history? In Ireland, the majority --
probably quite unhistorically -- refer their sense of a common origin to a
particular wave of early Celtic settlers in the island in pre-Christian
times, while the Protestant-Unionist community in the North generally refer theirs to the settlements and religious-political wars of the seventeenth
century.

No section of the Irish population today can afford to assert its identity in such terms as these, if to do so means excluding another section or
regarding it as alien. Ireland's greatest need today is that all who live in
the island should live and work in harmony. I quote once more from Parnell: "No, Sir; we cannot give up a single Irishman. We want the energy,
the patriotism, the talents, and the work of every Irishman."

An English observer in Ireland more than 300 years ago remarked
that: "In kingdoms conquered, nothing but time, and that also must be the
flux of hundreds of years, has power to unite the conqueror's issue and the
ancient inhabitants in perfect amity." In Ireland time has passed. But we
see now that Lloyd George's solution did not ease, but rather blocked, the
effect of its flux. It was a solution which seemed to him to respond best to
the exigencies of British politics at the time -- which had earlier encouraged intransigence on the part of a minority in Ireland. But, based as it
was on such considerations, it was unlikely to meet the best long-term interests of both islands. It is obvious now that it has not done so. In face
of its evident failure, the British government today must respond to the
real and pressing imperative -- which is to encourage and assist a settlement among Irishmen about Ireland, and not to obstruct it nor to be merely
neutral about it.

Source: Census Reports and Statistical Abstracts for the years in question, published by the Governments of Great Britain, Northern Ireland, and the Republic of Ireland.

THE PROVINCES AND COUNTIES OF IRELAND

Province of Connaught

	Area (sq. mi.)	County Town
Galway	2, 293	Galway
Letrim	589	Carrick on Shannon
Mayo	2, 084	Castlebar
Roscommon	951	Roscommon
Sligo	694	Sligo

Province of Leinster

Carlow	346	Carlow
Dublin	356	Dublin
Kildare	654	Naas
Kilkenny	796	Kilkenny
Leix (Laoighis)	664	Maryborough
Longford	403	Longford
Louth	317	Dundalk
Meath	903	Trim
Offaly	771	Tullamore
Westmeath	681	Mullingar
Wexford	908	Wexford
Wicklow	782	Wicklow

Province of Munster

Clare	1, 231	Ennis
Cork	2, 881	Cork
Kerry	1, 815	Tralee
Limerick	1, 037	Limerick
Tipperary	1, 643	Clonmel
Waterford	710	Waterford

Province of Ulster

Cavan	730	Cavan
Donegal	1, 865	Lifford
Monaghan	498	Monaghan

- - - - - - - - - - - - - -

Northern Ireland

Antrim	1, 122	Belfast
Armagh	489	Armagh
Down	952	Downpatrick
Fermanagh	653	Enniskillen
Londonderry	804	Londonderry
Tyrone	1, 218	Omagh

TOTAL AREA: 31, 840 sq. mi. (26, 602, Republic; 5, 238, N.I.).

POPULATION TRENDS IN IRELAND

Date	"26 Counties"	"6 Counties"	All Ireland
1831	6, 193, 197	1, 574, 004	7, 767, 401
1841	6, 528, 799	1, 646, 325	8, 175, 124
1881	3, 870, 020	1, 304, 8 16	5, 174, 836
1901	3, 221, 823	1, 236, 952	4, 458, 775
1926	2, 971, 992	1, 356, 561	4, 328, 553
1946	2, 955, 107	1, 334, 168	4, 289, 275
1961	2, 8 18, 341	1, 427, 000	4, 245, 341
1970 (UNO est.)	2, 944, 000	1, 524, 000	4, 468, 000

Assuming the maintenance of emigration at its present low level (through
economic expansion and the availability of employment), the UNO projects
(1966) a population of 3.34 million in the Republic by 1980.

OVERSEAS EMIGRATION DURING THE FAMINE ERA

1841	16, 000
1842	90, 000
1843	38, 000
1844	54, 000
1845	75, 000
1846	106, 000
1847	215, 000
1848	178, 000
1849	214, 000
1850	209, 000
1851	250, 000
1852	220, 000
1853	193, 000
1854	150, 000
1855	79, 000

These figures, which have been rounded to the nearest thousand, are de-
rived from British Census and Emigration Reports of the period, and, due
to anomalies in calculation, are approximately 5% below the actual total
emigration. During this period, between two-thirds and three-quarters
of each year's emigrants went to the United States. In 1851, over 86% did
so.

RELIGIOUS AFFILIATIONS IN IRELAND

<u>Republic of Ireland</u>

Catholics	2,768,033
Episcopalians	124,829
Presbyterians	23,870
Methodists	8,355
Jews	3,907
Baptists	462
Others & not stated	7,651

<u>Northern Ireland</u>

Catholics	497,547 (34.9%)
Presbyterians	413,113 (29.0%)
Episcopalians	344,800 (24.2%)
Methodists	71,865 (5.0%)
Brethren	16,847 (1.2%)
Baptists	13,765 (1.0%)
Congregationalists	9,838 (0.7%)
Unitarians	5,613 (0.4%)
Others	23,236 (1.6%)
Not stated	28,418 (2.0%)

These figures are based upon the latest available official data for religious affiliations (1961 Census and Statistical Abstract Reports). The proportional distribution has remained essentially the same over the past several decades.

The following list of works relating to the history of Ireland presents no more than a representative sampling of the available literature. With few exceptions, it does not include printed source material, or articles in learned journals and periodicals.

GENERAL WORKS

Arnold, Bruce. A Concise History of Irish Art, New York: Praeger, 1968.

Bailey, K. C. A History of Trinity College, Dublin, 1892-1945, Dublin: Dublin University Press, 1947.

Beckett, J. C. The Making of Modern Ireland, 1603-1923, London: Faber and Faber, 1966.

------------ A Short History of Ireland, London: Hutchison, 1966.

Chart, D. A. The Economic History of Ireland, Dublin: Talbot Press, 1920.
Cullen, L. M. Life in Ireland, London: Batsford, 1968.

Curtis, Edmund. A History of Ireland, 6th ed., London: Methuen, 1950.

Dowling, P. J. A History of Irish Education, Cork: Mercier, 1971.

Evans, E. E. Irish Folkways, London: Routledge & Kegan Paul, 1957.

Freeman, T. W. Ireland: A General and Regional Geography, 3rd ed., London: Methuen, 1965.

------------ Pre-Famine Ireland: A Study in Historical Geography, London: Methuen, 1957.

Hayes-McCoy, G. A. Irish Battles: A Military History of Ireland, London: Longmans, Green & Co., 1969.

Hyde, Douglas. A Literary History of Ireland . . ., London: T. F. Unwin, 1899.

Leask, H. G. Irish Castles and Castellated Houses, Dundalk: Dundalgan Press, 1941.

------------ Irish Churches and Monastic Buildings, 3 vols., Dundalk: Dundalgan Press, 1955-60.

Maxwell, Constantia. A History of Trinity College, Dublin, 1591-1892,

Dublin: Dublin University Press, 1946.

Moody, T. W. and Martin, F. X. (eds.). The Course of Irish History, Cork: Mercier, 1967.

Murray, A. E. A History of the Commercial and Financial Relations between England and Ireland from the Period of the Restoration, London: P. S. King & Son, 1903.

ANCIENT AND MEDIEVAL IRELAND

Armstrong, Olive. Edward Bruce's Invasion of Ireland, London: J. Murray, 1923.

Bieler, Ludwig. The Life and Legend of St. Patrick: Problems of Modern Scholarship, Dublin: Clonmore & Reynolds, 1949.

Bryan, Donough. The Great Earl of Kildare, Dublin: Talbot Press, 1933.

Carney, James. The Problem of St. Patrick, Dublin: Dublin Institute for Advanced Studies, 1961.

Chadwick, N. K. The Age of the Saints in the Early Celtic Church, London: Oxford University Press, 1961.

Conway, Agnes. Henry VII's Relations with Scotland and Ireland, Cambridge: Cambridge University Press, 1932.

Curtis, Edmund. A History of Medieval Ireland, from 1086 to 1513, 2nd ed., London: Methuen, 1938.

de Paor, Maire and Liam. Early Christian Ireland, London: Thames and Hudson, 1958.

Dillon, Myles (ed.). Early Irish Society, Dublin: Cultural Relations Committee, 1954.

Haliday, Charles. The Scandinavian Kingdom of Dublin, Dublin: M. H. Gill, 1882.

Hughes, Kathleen. The Church in Early Irish Society, Ithaca, N.Y.: Cornell University Press, 1966.

Jackson, K. H. The Oldest Irish Tradition, Cambridge: Cambridge University Press, 1964.

Murphy, Gerard. Saga and Myth in Ancient Ireland, Dublin: Cultural Relations Committee, 1955.

O'Riorain, S. P. Antiquities of the Irish Countryside, 4th ed., London: Methuen, 1964.

Orpen, G. H. Ireland Under the Normans, 1169-1333, 4 vols., Oxford: Clarendon Press, 1911-20.

Otway-Ruthven, A. J. A History of Medieval Ireland, London: Ernest Benn, Ltd., 1970.

Richardson, H. G., and Sayles, G. O. The Irish Parliament in the Middle Ages, Philadelphia: University of Pennsylvania Press, 1966.

Ryan, John. Irish Monasticism: Origins and Early Development, London: Longmans, Green & Co., 1931.

EARLY MODERN IRELAND

Bagwell, Richard. Ireland Under the Tudors, 3 vols., London: Longmans, Green & Co., 1885-90.
------------ Ireland Under the Stuarts, 3 vols., London: Longmans, Green & Co., 1909-16.
Beckett, J. C. Protestant Dissent in Ireland, 1687-1780, London: Faber and Faber, 1948.
Clarke, Aidan. The Old English in Ireland, 1625-42, Ithaca, N.Y.: Cornell University Press, 1966.

Corkery, Daniel. The Hidden Ireland: A Study of Gaelic Munster in the Eighteenth Century, Dublin: M. H. Gill & Son, 1967.
Edwards, R. Dudley. Church and State in Tudor Ireland, London: Longmans, Green & Co., 1935.

Falls, Cyril. Elizabeth's Irish Wars, London: Methuen, 1950.

Ferguson, Oliver W. Jonathan Swift and Ireland, Ubana, Ill., 1962.

Froude, J. A. The English in Ireland in the Eighteenth Century, 3 vols., 2nd ed., London: Longmans, Green & Co., 1881.

Gwynn, Stephen. Henry Grattan and His Times, London: Barnes and Noble, 1939.

Hayes, Richard. The Last Invasion of Ireland, 2nd ed., Dublin: M. H. Gill & Son, 1939.

Hogan, James. Ireland in the European System, London: Longmans, Green & Co., 1920.

Jacob, Rosamund. The Rise of the United Irishmen, 1791-94, London: George G. Harrap, 1937.

James, Francis G. Ireland in the Empire, 1688-1770. Cambridge, Mass.:
     Harvard University Press, 1973.

Johnston, Edith M. Great Britain and Ireland, 1760-1800: A Study in
     Political Administration, Edinburgh: 1963.

Kearney, H. F. Strafford in Ireland, 1633-41, Manchester: Manchester
     University Press, 1959.

Lecky, W. E. H. History of Ireland in the Eighteenth Century, 5 vols.,
     London: Longmans, Green & Co., 1892.

MacDermot, Frank. Theobald Wolfe Tone: A Biographical Study, London:
     Macmillan, 1939.

McDowell, R. B. Irish Public Opinion, 1750-1800, London: Faber & Faber,
     1944.

MacLysaght, Edward. Irish Life in the Seventeenth Century. . ., 2nd ed.,
     Cork: Cork University Press, 1950.

Maxwell, Constantia. Country and Town in Ireland Under the Georges,
     London: George G. Harrap, 1940.

———————— Dublin Under the Georges, 1714-1830, rev. ed., London:
     Faber and Faber, 1956.

Meehan, C. P. The Confederation of Kilkenny, Dublin: J. Duffy, 1905.

Moody, T. W. The Londonderry Plantation, Belfast: W. Mullan & Son,
     1939.

O'Brien, George. The Economic History of Ireland in the Seventeenth
     Century, Dublin: Maunsel & Co., 1919.

———————— The Economic History of Ireland in the Eighteenth Century,
     Dublin: Maunsel & Co., 1918.

O'Connell, Maurice R. Irish Politics and Social Conflict in the Age of
     the American Revolution, Philadelphia: University of Pennsyl-
     vania Press, 1965.

Prendergast, J. P. The Cromwellian Settlement of Ireland, New York:
     Haverty, 1868.

Quinn, D. B. The Elizabethans and the Irish, Ithaca, N.Y.: Cornell Uni-
     versity Press, 1966.

Rogers, Patrick. The Volunteers and Catholic Emancipation, 1778-93,
     London: Burns, Oates & Washbourne, 1934.

Senior, Hereward. Orangeism in Ireland and Britain, 1795-1836, London: Routledge & Kegan Paul, 1966.

Silke, J. J. Kinsale: The Spanish Intervention in Ireland at the End of the Elizabethan Wars, Liverpool: Liverpool University Press, 1970.

Simms, J. G. The Jacobite War in Ireland, London: Routlege & Kegan Paul, 1969.

------------ The Williamite Confiscation in Ireland, 1690-1703, London: Faber and Faber, 1958.

Wall, Maureen. The Penal Laws, 1691-1760, Dundalk: Dublin Historical Association, 1961.

IRELAND SINCE THE UNION

Adams, W. F. Ireland and Irish Emigration to the New World from 1815 to the Famine, New Haven: Yale University Press, 1932.

Akenson, D. H. The Church of Ireland: Ecclesiastical Reform and Revolution, 1800-1885, New Haven: Yale University Press, 1971.

Ayearst, Morley. The Republic of Ireland: Its Government and Politics, London: George Allen & Unwin, 1971.

Bromage, Mary C. De Valera and the March of a Nation, London: Hutchinson, 1956.

Chart, D. A. Ireland from the Union to Catholic Emancipation, London: J. M. Dent & Sons, 1910.

Chubb, Basil. The Government and Politics of Ireland, Stanford, Cal.: Stanford University Press, 1970.

Colum, Padraic. Arthur Griffith, Dublin: Browne & Nolan, 1959.

Coogan, T. P. Ireland Since the Rising, New York: Praeger, 1966.

Curtis, L. P. Coercion and Conciliation in Ireland, 1880-92, Princeton: Princeton University Press, 1963.

Davitt, Michael. The Fall of Feudalism in Ireland, or the Story of the Land League Revolution, London: Harper, 1904.

de Paor, Liam. Divided Ulster, Baltimore: Penguin Books, 1971.

Edwards, R. Dudley, and Williams, T. D. (eds.). The Great Famine: Studies in Irish History, 1845-52, Dublin: Browne and Nolan, 1956.

FitzGibbon, Constantine. Red Hand: The Ulster Colony, Garden City, N.Y.:
          Doubleday, 1971.

Greaves, C. D. The Life and Times of James Connolly, London: Lawrence
          and Wishart, 1961.
Green, E. R. R. The Lagan Valley, 1800-1850: A Local History of the
          Industrial Revolution, London: Faber and Faber, 1949.

Gwynn, Denis. The Life of John Redmond, London, 1932.
------------ Young Ireland and 1848, Cork: Cork University Press,
          1949.

Hammond, J. L. Gladstone and the Irish Nation, new ed., London: Long-
          mans, Green & Co., 1964.

Kee, Robert The Green Flag. The Turbulent History of the Irish National
          Movement. New York: Delacorte Press, 1972.
Larkin, Emmet. James Larkin, Irish Labour Leader, 1876-1947. London:
          Routledge & Kegan Paul, 1965.

Lyons, F. S. L. Ireland Since the Famine, 1850 to the Present, London:
          Weidenfeld & Nicolson, 1971.

------------ The Fall of Parnell, 1890-91, London: Routledge & Kegan
          Paul, 1960.
------------ The Irish Parliamentary Party, 1890-1910, London: Faber
          and Faber, 1951.

McCaffrey, L. J. Daniel O'Connell and the Repeal Year, Lexington, Ky.:
          University of Kentucky Press, 1966.

McCracken, J. L. Representative Government in Ireland: A Study of Dail
          Eireann, 1919-48, London: Oxford University Press, 1958.
McDowell, R. B. Public Opinion and Government Policy in Ireland, 1801-
          1846, London: Faber and Faber, 1952.

Macintyre, Angus. The Liberator: Daniel O'Connell and the Irish Party,
          1830-1847, London: Macmillan, 1965.

Manning, Maurice. The Blueshirts, Toronto: University of Toronto Press,
          1971.

Mansergh, Nicholas. The Irish Question, 1840-1921, new ed., London:
          George Allen & Unwin, 1965.

Marjoribanks, Edward, and Colvin, Ian. The Life of Lord Carson, 3 vols.,
          London: Gollanez, 1932-36.
Neeson, Eoin. The Civil War in Ireland, 1921-23, Cork: Mercier, 1966.

Norman, E. R. The Catholic Church and Ireland in the Age of Rebellion,
          1859-73, London: Longmans, Green & Co., 1965.

Nowlan, Kevin. The Politics of Repeal; A Study in the Relations between
          Great Britain and Ireland, 1841-50, London: Routledge and
          Kegan Paul, 1965.

O'Brien, C. C. Parnell and His Party, 1880-90, new ed., Oxford: Claredon
          Press, 1964.

O'Broin, Leon. The Unfortunate Mr Robert Emmet, Dublin: Clonmore &
          Reynolds, 1958.

O'Faolain, Sean. King of the Beggars, A Life of Daniel O'Connell . . .
          London: T. Nelson & Sons, 1938.

O'Leary, John. Recollections of Fenians and Fenianism, 2 vols., London:
          Downey, 1896.

O'Sullivan, Donal. The Irish Free State and its Senate, London: Faber
          and Faber, 1940.

Pakenham, Frank. Peace by Ordeal, new ed., London: John Cape, 1962.

Pearse, P. H. Political Writings and Speeches, Dublin: Maunsel & Roberts,
          1922.

Reynolds, James. The Catholic Emancipation Crisis in Ireland, 1823-29,
          New Haven: Yale University Press, 1954.

Ryan, A. P. Mutiny at the Curragh, London: Macmillan, 1956.

Ryan, Desmond. The Rising: The Complete Story of Easter Week, 3rd ed.,
          Dublin: Golden Eagle Books, 1957.

Shearman, Hugh. Not an Inch: A Study of Northern Ireland and Lord
          Craigavon, London: Faber & Faber, 1942.

Schrier, Arnold. Ireland and the American Emigration, 1850-1900, Min-
          neapolis: University of Minnesota Press, 1958.

Tierney, Michael (ed.). Daniel O'Connell: Nine Centenary Essays, Dublin:
          Browne and Nolan, 1949.

Thornley, D. A. Isaac Butt and Home Rule, London: Macgibbon & Kee, 1964.

Wallace, Martin. *Northern Ireland: 50 Years of Self Government.* Devon,
       1971.

Whyte, J. H. *The Independent Irish Party, 1850-59.* London: Oxford Uni-
       versity Press, 1958.

Williams, T. D. (ed.). *The Irish Struggle, 1916-26.* London: Routledge &
       Kegan Paul, 1966.

PERIODICALS

A broad range of Irish historical topics is covered in *Irish His-
torical Studies*, the joint journal of the Irish Historical Society and the
Ulster Society for Irish Historical Studies. For the earlier period, such
journals as *Studia Hibernica*, the *Proceedings of the Royal Irish Academy*,
and the *Journal of the Royal Society of Antiquaries of Ireland* are valuable.
In addition, there are regional publications, such as the *Dublin Historical
Record*, the *Ulster Journal of Archaeology*, and the journals of the Cork,
Galway, and Louth archaelogical and historical societies. Religious history
is emphasized in the *Proceedings of the Irish Catholic Historical Committee* and the *Irish Ecclesiastical Record*, while the military history of
Ireland and of the Irish abroad is dealt with in *The Irish Sword*, the journal
of the Military History Society of Ireland. The monthly review *Hibernia*
seeks to present a comprehensive examination of contemporary Irish
society and its problems.

The principal newspapers in the Republic are *The Irish Times*, *The
Irish Press* (complemented by the *Sunday Press*), and the *Irish Indepen-
dent* (linked with the *Sunday Independent* and the *Evening Herald*) -- all
published in Dublin. In the North, there are the *Belfast Telegraph*, the
News Letter (published in Belfast since 1737), and the nationalist *Irish
News*.

NORTH COUNTRY LIBRARY SYSTEM
0 11 01 0087060 6